## AFRICAN HISTORICAL DICTIONARIES
### Edited by Jon Woronoff

1. *Cameroon*, by Victor T. LeVine and Roger P. Nye. 1974
2. *The Congo (Brazzaville)*, by Virginia Thompson and Richard Adloff. 1974
3. *Swaziland*, by John J. Grotpeter. 1975
4. *The Gambia*, by Harry A. Gailey. 1975
5. *Botswana*, by Richard P. Stevens. 1975
6. *Somalia*, by Margaret F. Castagno. 1975
7. *Dahomey*, by Samuel Decalo. 1975
8. *Burundi*, by Warren Weinstein. 1976
9. *Togo*, by Samuel Decalo. 1976
10. *Lesotho*, by Gordon Haliburton. 1977
11. *Mali*, by Pascal James Imperato. 1977
12. *Sierra Leone*, by Cyril Patrick Foray. 1977
13. *Chad*, by Samuel Decalo. 1977
14. *Upper Volta*, by Daniel Miles McFarland. 1978
15. *Tanzania*, by Laura S. Kurtz. 1978
16. *Guinea*, by Thomas O'Toole. 1978
17. *Sudan*, by John Voll. 1978

# Historical Dictionary
## of
# GUINEA
### (Republic of Guinea/Conakry)

by

## THOMAS E. O'TOOLE

*African Historical Dictionaries, No. 16*

## The Scarecrow Press, Inc.
## Metuchen, N.J. & London
## 1978

Library of Congress Cataloging in Publication Data

O'Toole, Thomas, 1941-
    Historical dictionary of Guinea (Republic of Guinea/
Conakry).

    (African historical dictionaries ; no. 16)
    Bibliography: p.
    1.  Guinea--History--Dictionaries.   2.   Guinea--
Bibliography.  I.  Title.  II.  Series.
DT543.5.O88              966'.52'005              77-28145
ISBN 0-8108-1112-X

ii

for
Ann, Rachel and Phillip
with love

# ACKNOWLEDGMENT

I have to thank a number of people for making this book possible. In the first place my wife, Ann, was devoted and tireless in preparation of the bibliography. My daughter, Rachel and son Phillip, bore up well to life with an often preoccupied father. Professor Ed Cohen and Ms. Naja Williams of Hunter Library at Western Carolina University were most helpful. Two other friends also gave invaluable assistance. Janice Baker, a former resident of Guinea, now at the Library of Congress, helped me in checking post-1970 materials. A Guinean friend, Dr. Lansinê Kaba, now at the University of Minnesota, gave considerable insight into the present-day actualities in Guinea. Finally Lynda Morgan, Cathy Elrod, Susan Gordon Reid and Sharon Rothrock at Western Carolina University aided in arranging the bibliography and typing the manuscript.

T. O.


Cullowhee, North Carolina
May, 1977

# CONTENTS

# EDITOR'S FOREWORD

Few African countries entered independent nationhood with such great promise as Guinea, and few leaders aroused an enthusiasm as great and wide-spread as Sékou Touré. The first Black African colony to break its bonds with France, its first leader to resolutely embrace nonalignment, and the first regime to openly proclaim socialism, Sékou Touré's Guinea appeared as a natural leader to many, especially among the young and radical.

Two decades later, independence, non-alignment, and socialism are still proclaimed stridently and broadly, and have even been implemented ... in a Guinean fashion. But there is no echo. Guinea's experiment has hardly been a success in the eyes of its detractors, its competitors, and even often in its own terms. But its biggest failure would seem to be that neither its supporters nor its opponents take it seriously any more. Guinea has ceased being a model and become a backwater, remembered only after some spectacular and, more often than not, violent event.

What then has been happening in one of Africa's once best-known countries, now hardly possible to stay informed about even through the specialized press and journals? Collecting the information was not an easy task, despite the author's familiarity with Guinea. And telling this story without the blind optimism or the disgust that often color much of the writing about, or from, Guinea is indeed an achievement.

Dr. Thomas O'Toole went to Guinea with the Peace Corps for about two years in 1963-1965, one of the most exciting periods in modern African history, when unity appeared around the corner and fraternity had a deep meaning. These were also years when Sékou Touré's thought and action influenced much of the continent. Since then, through personal contacts and other sources, he has continued to follow the country's more somber path. Expanding on a short book and his Encyclopaedia Britannica entry on Guinea, Dr. O'Toole in this dictionary gives us a rare glimpse of the present situation.

Jon Woronoff
Series Editor

# NOTE ON SPELLING

We are far from possessing a standard orthography
for most of the indigenous languages of Guinea and only since
independence has there been any real attempt to standardize
spellings. The fact that French, Portuguese and English
variants for many terms exist along with different forms in
the various African languages of Guinea only compounds the
difficulty.

A single ethnic group, the Fulbê, can be labeled Peul,
Fula or Fulani depending on the source. Since Peul is the
singular and Fulbê is the plural used by Fulfuldê (Fulbê
speakers) for members of this ethnic group, they will be
identified herein as Fulbê.

Generally agreed spellings of names and terms will
usually be used even when they are not linguistically correct.
When widely divergent spelling varieties exist the various
forms will generally be given, with the most common term
given first.

# ABBREVIATIONS AND ACRONYMS

| | |
|---|---|
| Afrimar | Société Africaine des Pêches Maritimes |
| AGF | Association des Guinéens en France |
| AGP | Agence Guinéenne de Presse |
| AOF | Afrique Occidentale Française |
| BAG | Bloc Africain de Guinée |
| BCEAO | Banque Centrale des Etats de l'Afrique de l'Ouest |
| BCRG | Banque Centrale de la République de Guinée |
| BGCE | Banque Guinéene de Commerce Extérieur |
| BNDA | Banque Nationale pour de Développement Agricole |
| BPN | Bureau Politique National |
| CAP | Coopérative Agricole de Production |
| CBG | Compagnie de Bauxites de Guinée |
| CC | Comité Central |
| CER | Centre d'Education Révolutionnaire |
| CFA | Communauté Financière Africaine |
| CFAO | Compagnie Française de l'Afrique Occidentale |
| CGCE | Comptoir Guinéen du Commerce Extérieur |
| CGCI | Comptoir Guinéen du Commerce Intérieur |
| CGT | Confédération Général du Travail |
| CMR | Centre de Modernisation Rurale |
| CNE | Caisse Nationale d'Epargne |
| CNF | Comité National des Femmes |
| CNPA | Centre National de Production Agricole |
| CNR | Conseil National de la Révolution |
| CNTG | Confédération Nationale des Travailleurs Guinéens |
| COPAC | Coopérative de Production Agricole et de Consommation |
| CUP | Comité d'Unité de Production |
| DSG | Démocratic Socialiste de Guinée |
| ESA | Ecole Supérieure d'Administration |
| FEANF | Fédération des Etudiants de l'Afrique Noire en France |
| FIDES | Fonds d'Investissement pour le Développement Economique |

| | |
|---|---|
| FLNG | Front pour la Libération Nationale de Guinée |
| HALCO | a consortium formed by Harvey Aluminum Company |
| IBA | Association Inter-Gouvernementale des Pays Producteurs de Bauxite |
| IFAN | Institut Français d'Afrique Noire |
| INRD | Institut National de Recherches et de Documentation |
| IPC | Institut Polytechnique Gamal Abdel Nasser de Conakry |
| JORG | Journal Officiel de la République de Guinée |
| JRDA | Jeunesse de la Révolution Démocratique Africaine |
| MIFERGUI | Société des Mines de Fer de Guinée |
| OAU | Organization of African Unity |
| OCA | Office de Commercialisation Agricole |
| ONCFG | Office National des Chemins de Fer de Guinée |
| PAIGC | Partido Africão da Independência da Guiné e do Cabo-Verde |
| PDG | Parti Démocratique de Guinée |
| PPG | Parti Progressiste de Guinée |
| PRC | People's Republic of China |
| PRL | Pouvoir Révolutionnaire Local |
| PZ | Paterson-Zochonis |
| RDA | Rassemblement Démocratique Africain |
| SCOA | Société Commerciale de l'Ouest Africain |
| SFIO | Section Française de l'Internationale Ouvrière |
| SIAG | Société Industrielle et Automobile de Guinée |
| SIP | Société Indigène de Prévoyance |
| SNA | Société Nationale d'Assurance |
| SOGUIP | Société Guinéenne de Pétrole |
| Sonigue | Société Nippo-Guinéenne de Pêche |
| Soguikop | Société Guinéo-Koweitienne de Pêche |
| UGTAN | Union Générale des Travailleurs d'Afrique Noire |

# CHRONOLOGICAL LIST OF MAJOR EVENTS

| | |
|---|---|
| 920-1050 | Guinea is part of Empire of Ghana |
| ca. 1235-1255 | Sundiata Keita, King of Mali |
| 1240 | Sundidata destroys Ghana |
| 1307-1332 | Kankan Mansa Musa, ruler of Mali |
| 1324 | Kankan Mansa Musa's pilgrimage to Mecca |
| 1470 | Benedetto Dei, a Florentine, visits Timbuktu |
| early 1500's | Fulbé begin to arrive on the Futa Jalon plateau |
| 1513 | 505 slaves sent from Guinea to Portugal |
| 1514 | 978 slaves sent from Guinea to Portugal |
| post-1542 | French privateers active on the Guinea coast and attack Fogos Island |
| 1594 | Moroccan army ends Songhai Empire |
| ca. 1622 | 3000 slaves sent annually from Guinea to Portugal |
| July 1687 | English factory established at Rio Núñez |
| 1714 | French Senegal Co. sets up factories on the Guinea Coast |
| ca. 1725 | Karamoko Alfa and Ibrahima Sori began Jihad in Futa Jalon |
| 1768 | Moravian missionaries arrive on Guinea coast |
| 1795-1797 | Mungo Park reaches Ségu and the Niger from Gambia |
| ca. 1800 | Muslim state fully established in Futa Jalon |
| 1808 | British establish a naval patrol against slave traders in West African waters |

| 1824-1826 | René Caillé leaves Senegal to explore to Timbuktu |
| 1842 | French treaties with Landouma and Nalou leaders in Guinea |
| ca. 1850 | Al Hajj Umar attacks Bambara kingdoms of Ségou and Kaarta from Dinguiraye in the Futa Jalon |
| 1854 | the jihad of Al Hajj Umar begins |
| Aug.-Sept. 1860 | French force Al Hajj Umar to retire to the Niger |
| 1866 | France acquires trading centers on Guinea coast |
| 1868 | French posts established at Boké and Benty |
| 1880 | French obtain railway concession in Guinea from some Fulbé leaders |
| 1881-1899 | French expeditions against Samory Touré |
| June 28, 1882 | Anglo-French agreement on Sierra Leone and Guinea boundaries |
| May 12, 1885 | Franco-Portuguese Convention on Portuguese Guinea and French Guinea boundaries |
| 1890-1894 | French explorations in Guinea |
| March 10, 1893 | French colony of Guinea is officially established |
| June 15, 1895 | AOF established |
| April 8, 1904 | a further Anglo-French convention on French Guinea boundaries |
| Nov. 5, 1904 | Franco-Portuguese treaty on Guinea boundaries |
| 1905 | a number of anti-colonial struggles in French Guinea are in progress |
| Sept. 18, 1907 | Franco-Liberia agreement on Liberian-French Guinea borders |
| Dec. 4, 1920 | AOF reorganized |
| March 30, 1925 | Africans are elected to Conseils d'Administration in Guinea |
| Dec. 7, 1942 | AOF joins the Allies |

| | |
|---|---|
| Jan. 30-Feb. 8, 1944 | Brazzaville Conference |
| Nov. 4, 1945 | Yaciné Diallo from Guinea elected to represent AOF in French constituent assembly |
| April 11, 1946 | corvée abolished in AOF |
| May 7, 1946 | French citizenship with a limited franchise given all AOF subjects |
| Oct. 18, 1946 | RDA founded in Bamako with PDG as a section |
| 1952 | Sékou Touré becomes Secretary-General of the Guinea branch of the RDA |
| 1956 | PDG-RDA sweeps elections as Sékou Touré is returned to National Assembly in Paris |
| Sept. 28, 1958 | Guineans reject De Gaulle constitution by 1,136,324 to 56,981 votes |
| Oct. 2, 1958 | Guinea becomes an independent republic, with Sékou Touré as President |
| Jan. 15, 1961 | nationalization program starts with takeover of power and water supplies |
| Nov. 1961 | "Teacher's Plot" put down; Daniel Solod, Soviet Ambassador, expelled |
| Nov. 22, 1965 | diplomatic relations with France broken off following October plot allegedly backed by French |
| March 2, 1966 | Kwame Nkrumah of Ghana offered asylum and offered honorary co-presidency |
| Feb. 1969 | the "Labé plot": 13 sentenced to death, 27 imprisoned for plotting against Sékou Touré |
| June 24, 1969 | assassination attempt on Sékou Touré during visit of President Kenneth Kaunda of Zambia |
| Nov. 2, 1970 | Portuguese and Guinean exiles try to take Conakry; they fail, 92 are condemned to death and 66 to hard labor for life |
| Jan. 24, 1971 | diplomatic relations broken with Senegal, and on Jan. 29, 1971, with West Germany, on grounds that they had taken part in abortive Conakry invasion |

| | |
|---|---|
| Feb. 1971 | series of visits from heads of states starts with President Ngouabi of Congo-Brazzaville |
| April, 1972 | President Sékou Touré unanimously re-elected president at the PDG's Ninth Congress |
| May 9, 1975 | diplomatic relations with West Germany resume after a five-year lapse |
| July 14, 1975 | diplomatic relations with France resume |
| July, 1975 | Touré makes state visits to Upper Volta and Mali |
| Jan. 1976 | Guinea agrees to participate in the Second World Black and African Festival of Arts and Culture in Lagos |
| Sept. 1977 | Touré interprets Koran as supporting the PDG on Guinean radio |

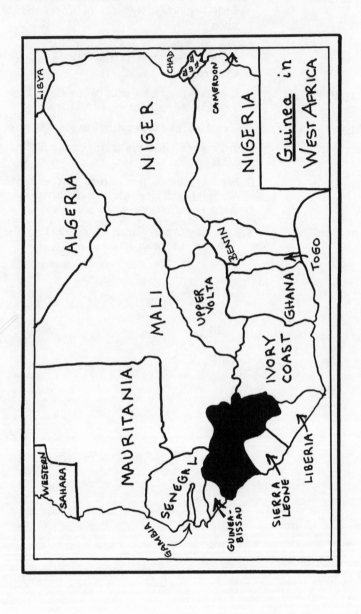

# INTRODUCTION

The origin of the name Guinea itself is obscure. Some suggest that Guinea might be derived from the ancient Niger Basin trading center, Jenné. More likely it derives, through Portuguese usage, from the Berber Akal-n-Iguinawen or "Land of the Blacks." Yet another possibility is that it comes from the word geenay, meaning "women" among the coastal Susu, and somehow this name came to be applied to a widespread area of the African coast.

The modern Republic of Guinea faces southwest to the Atlantic on the western extension of Africa between 8° and 12° north latitude. Guinea touches on six other African nations; clockwise north to south they are Guinea-Bissau, Senegal, Mali, Ivory Coast, Liberia, and Sierra Leone. Guinea is traditionally divided into four natural regions: (1) Lower Guinea (the coastal areas); (2) Middle Guinea which consists chiefly of the highlands of the Futa-Jalon, inland from the sea; (3) Upper Guinea, which descends gradually northwest towards the Sahara desert; and (4) the Forest region which stands astride the watershed between the Niger river drainage plains and southward flowing rivers which exit to the Atlantic through Liberia and Sierra Leone.

Climatically all of Guinea shares two alternating seasons: a dry season (November to March) and a wet season (April to October). Rainfall varies from region to region with as much as 170 inches a year at Conakry on the coast to less than 60 inches a year in Upper Guinea. The rainfall in Middle Guinea ranges from 63 to 91 inches a year while some areas in the Forest Region have more than 100 inches of rain a year. Temperate ranges also vary according to the different regions. On the coast and in the forest region the temperature ranges around an average of 81° Fahrenheit. While the Futa highland of Middle Guinea may experience January daytime temperatures from 86°F to 95°F nightime temperatures may dip below 50°F. Midday highs of more than 100°F are not uncommon in Upper Guinea during the dry season.

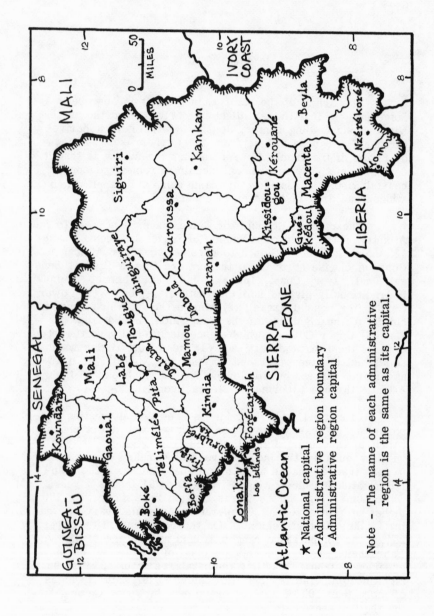

The natural drainage system includes the Niger River
and its two main tributaries, the Tinkisso and the Milo in
Upper Guinea.   In the Futa highlands both the Senegal and
the Gambia have their sources as well as the Rio Núñez,
Konkouré, Fatala and the Melikouré, which flow southwest
to the Atlantic.   Flowing more southerly through Sierra
Leone and Liberia a number of minor rivers drain the Forest Region boundary area.

Most of Guinea is composed of savanna grasslands
and orchard shrub with soils largely composed of silicates
of aluminum hydrate except along rivers and the tidal areas.
Major food crops include millet, maize, rice, manioc (cas-
sava) and oil palms while some coffee and bananas are cultivated for export.

Guinea's estimated population of around five million
is composed of a variety of ethnic groups.   The present day
boundaries of Guinea were determined by colonial powers
with little regard to the ethnic or linguistic groupings of
African people.   These boundaries, therefore, often split
ethnic and linguistic groups.   Within the country, though, the
four major geographic regions largely correspond to four major ethnolinguistic groups.   In Lower Guinea Susu, a Manding language, closely related to the Dialonké language of
Middle Guinea, has largely replaced that of the Landoma,
Baga, Nalou and other West Atlantic languages once widely
spoken in the coastal areas.   In the Futa Jalon of Middle
Guinea the Fulbé language is dominant, although minor indigenous ethnic groups like the Badyaranké, Bassari and
Coniagui, and Manding speaking immigrants like the Dialonké
and Diakhanté continue to maintain some of their traditional
ways.   Maninkakan, the language of the Maninka, is widely
spoken in Upper Guinea, and has long been penetrating into
the Forest zone where three very different linguistic groups
still are dominant.   These three linguistic areas, from east
to west, are the Kpelle (Guerzé), Loma (Toma) and Kissi.
A number of other minor ethnic groups exist in Guinea but
the process of creating a national identity in Guinea has made
considerable headway since independence.   As President
Touré has suggested, ethnicity should not be denied but it
should also be obvious that no ethnic group will survive if
Guinea perishes because of inter-ethnic rivalries.   The
growth of the whole national community has largely taken
priority over ethnic particularism in Guinea.

Based on official Guinean census figures the popula-

tion density of Guinea in the early 1970's was almost 54 persons per square mile.    But given the nature of the slash-
and-burn subsistence farming which still prevails throughout
much of Guinea and the persistent need for the importation
of food, it is unlikely that these figures are very accurate.
The administrational regions of Labé and Pita in the Futa
Jalon, both having agreeable climate and fairly good soil
conditions, probably has over 100 persons per square mile.
In the forest region the rich agricultural areas around Guékédou and Nzérékoré may also have maintained populations in
excess of 90 persons per square mile.    But Upper Guinea,
encompassing two-fifths of Guinea's total territory, has about
27 people per square mile.    Except in fertile areas along the
Niger and Milo Rivers the large stretches of savanna and
savanna woodland in Upper Guinea are very lightly inhabited.
The Conakry, Dubréka and Fria regions in Lower Guinea have
more than doubled their population in the past twenty years
as bauxite mining, bauxite processing and other industries
have grown.    Conakry and its suburban environs on the Kaloum peninsula has over 4400 people per square mile, while
Fria and Dubré have more than 90.    It would seem that uneven urbanization of this sort could create social, political
and economic problems for Guinea in the future.

          The pre-colonial history of Guinea still remains rather
incomplete.    Though archeological research in Guinea has not
made much progress, evidence seems to indicate that the
area has been continuously inhabited by hunting-and-gathering
populations for at least the past 30,000 years.    It also seems
probable that farming has been practiced in the area of
Guinea for at least the past 3000 years.    There is considerable evidence that iron smelting dates back more than 2000
years in this part of West Africa.    But until further archeological evidence is forthcoming, much of the early history
of Guinea remains conjectural.

          The pre-colonial history of Guinea becomes much
clearer from about A.D. 900 as sources in Arabic and oral
traditions become available.    Travelers' accounts in Arabic
and professional history keepers' oral narratives offer information on the genealogies of royal families and traditions
of ethnic groups who lived in Guinea in the past millenium.
For peoples like the Coniagui, Baga, and Nalou, who now
live on the Atlantic coast, ethnological evidence supports the
view that they lived in the area of modern Guinea even before the Christian era.    Others, like the Susu and Maninka,
probably came into the area about A.D. 900, while the Fulbé

who arrived in large numbers in the 17th century, are almost newcomers.

Much of Upper Guinea's pre-colonial history is closely
tied to the three great centralized savanna states of West
Africa--Ghana, Mali, and Songhai--which dominated the lands
to the north and east of modern Guinea from about A.D. 1000
to the mid-16th century. Villages and small kingdoms of
the Maninka people located on the headwaters of the Niger
River began to achieve historical prominence in the 13th century. The gold fields of Buré near modern Siguiri greatly
contributed to the wealth of all the trade based empires of the
western savanna but were certainly very important to the Mali
Empire. Oral traditions maintain that the powerful empire
of Ghana, which dated from at least the eighth century, forced
the towns and villages of Upper Guinea to pay equal weights
in gold for the salt that had to pass through Ghana from desert mines in the north. Oral historians or griots maintain
that about A.D. 1235 a popular and effective leader, Sundiata Keita, united the various Maninka villages and groups and
defeated Sumanguru, an especially oppressive Susu war leader who had gained control of the old Ghana empire around
1200. Sundiata was probably born in a Maninka village inside Guinea's present boundaries.

With the decline of the Mali Empire in the late 14th
century new forces began to control the area of modern
Guinea. In the late 15th century, Coli Tenguela (or Temala),
a Fulbé leader, conquered the Futa Jalon with a small number of followers. Originally from the central Senegal River
valley, he passed through the Guinean towns of Timbo and
Labé in his conquest. Because much of Coli Tenguela's conquest was accomplished by using local populations as troops,
the number of Fulbé involved was never large. The only
long-term effect of these conquests was to push Susu and
Maninka groups to the coast where they often established
themselves as rulers over the local peoples.

These coastal areas were drawn into European market
systems from the mid-15th century on. Local rulers on the
coast began to grow in power by recruiting members to their
groups with the promise of imported trade goods. Though
not one of the major slave trading areas of West Africa,
Guinea was affected by the wars and disruption occasioned
by this trade. By the end of the slave trade in the early
19th century, European trade goods had replaced many types
of locally produced goods. Consequently the French and

British commercial interests which had achieved dominance
on the coast were poised to intervene even more deeply in
internal African affairs.

It should not be supposed, though, that British and
ultimately French trading interests played a very important
role in the Guinean interior before the mid-19th century.
At the end of the 17th century, increasing numbers of Fulbé
cattlekeepers had moved into the Futa Jalon. Upset at pay-
ing taxes to the non-Muslim residents of the area the Fulbé
created a theocratic Muslim state in the Futa Jalon. This
state itself was torn by internal dissent until the French oc-
cupied the Futa Jalon in 1897, but it firmly established the
Islamic theory of a God-ruled state in the minds of many
Guineans.

In 1826, a young Muslim religious leader from the
Futa Toro in upper Senegal returned to West Africa. This
man, Al Hajj Umar, settled in the Futa Jalon and began
teaching a simple, devout form of Islam--the Tijaniyya. Expelled from the Futa Jalon as a potential threat to the existing Muslim state, he fled to Dinguiraye near the Buré gold
fields in Upper Guinea. From there he gathered forces and
launched an attack on the Bambara states to the east. After
his death internal revolts and French pressures destroyed
his forces.

Not all African leaders were as easily defeated by
the French. Almany Samory Touré, a Guinean Maninka leader, had proposed alliance against the French with Umar's
son, Ahmad in 1883 or 1884. Though Ahmad defeated this
alliance, the story of Samory remains an important part of
Guinean history. The first president of Guinea, Ahmed
Sékou Touré, claimed descent from Samory and Guinean
school children are taught that Samory was a forerunner of
national independence because of his determined resistance to
the French. As the leader of an independent Maninka state
in southeast Guinea from 1882 until 1898, he did provide the
French with more military resistance than they had bargained
for. Unfortunately, the French had the greater sources of
supply. Samory was never able to obtain enough modern
weapons to resist the French in the long run. His efforts
at unification with other African leaders failed because these
other leaders did not see as clearly as he the growing threat
the French posed to African autonomy. Samory was captured
by the French in 1899 and exiled. Belatedly and in isolation,
small groups of Africans continued to resist the French until

the end of World War I but treaties with Great Britain and
Liberia had by then already established the boundaries of
colonial French Guinea.

French rule brought some important changes in the
social and political structure of African society.  Largescale African polities were replaced by a French administrative structure.  Private ownership of former communal land
and the expansion of commercial and service occupations re-
sulted in the development of civil servants, teachers, small
shops and plantation owners, medical and military personnel
and transportation.  Gradually an urban elite evolved which
adapted the French language and culture.  But the majority
of Africans continued to live in villages and practice subsistence agriculture well into the 1940s.

After World War II political activities among this
French educated elite grew.  Ethnic-based parties and affiliates of parties in France were to dominate.  In the 1950s
the Parti Démocratique de Guinée, a new labor-based party
founded in 1947, began to mobilize the support of the peasants, youth and women.  It was this party, under the leadership of Sékou Touré, that lead the Guinean people to vote
against General De Gaulle's proposed French Community in
the referendum on September 28, 1958.  On October 2, 1958,
Guinean independence was formally proclaimed.  Cut off
from budgetary assistance and the favored-nation status of
Guinean exports to France, faced with a shortage of trained
administrators, teachers, military staff and medical personnel, Guinea began independence with no resources other than
a highly enthusiastic and hopeful population.  The strong
unifying force of a charismatic leader and a popularly based
party in the early years of independence succeeded in over-
coming interpersonal conflicts, the difficulties of rising ex-
pectations among the small Guinean elite, ethnic cleavages
and the great lack of economic resources and infrastructure
for development.

Over the first ten years of independence, Guinea continued to occupy a special position among African states in
its unqualified rejection of colonial control or economic domination by more developed nations.  Taking a militant pan-
Africanist stance in African affairs, one of "positive-neutral-
ism" in the cold war, and combining a unique articulation of
African socialism and "cultural revolution" in internal affairs,
Guinea, under the leadership of Sékou Touré, presented an
image of radical experimentation in social and political de-

velopment in Africa.    Unfortunately the rate of economic development was rather slow and from 1960 on a number of
attempts have been made to overthrow the government of
Sékou Touré by assassination, coup d'état and invasion.

        In April 1960 a plot to overthrow the government by
armed force was alleged by PDG agents.    The instigators of
this plot were apparently Guinean citizens who resented the
anti-capitalist socialist thrust of the PDG regime.    In November 1961 Touré accused the Soviet embassy of supporting
a teacher's strike, which was crushed with considerable
severity.    In late 1965 leaders of a group seeking to form
an opposition party were arrested and charged with plotting
to bring about the downfall of Touré's government.    In February 1969 the army was purged along with other dissidents
in the Party and in June 1969 an apparent assassination attempt on Touré, blamed on an exile opposition group, was
almost successful.    In November 1970 a seaborne invasion
of the capital, Conakry, launched by Portuguese troops and
Guinean exiles proved abortive.    Another purge of the
Guinean political and administrative elite followed.    In July
1971 the army's officer corps was similarly purged and in
April 1973 a number of cabinet ministers were accused
by President Touré of plotting to overthrow his government.
Such purges and accusations have become increasingly com-
monplace in recent years.

        Guinean groups made up of pre-independence opponents
of the PDG, former PDG officials who have deserted the regime, professionals, businessmen, dissident military leaders,
ex-servicemen, academics and students along with migrant
Guinean traders and laborers do form substantial external
forces in opposition to Sékou Touré.    Based mainly in France,
Senegal and the Ivory Coast, they represent a number of factions and could possibly have played a role in some of the at-
tacks on President Touré and the present government of Guinea.    Internal opposition has been all but silenced.

        Smuggling and black-market activities continue to op-
erate to some extent as a result of the PDG regime's failure
to promote economic growth.    The majority of Guineans de-
sire a better standard of living, yet are probably quite proud
of the Guinean nation even though the rule of the PDG, supposedly a popular dictatorship based on the will of the people,
has become increasingly restrictive and centered in the person
of the "Doctor of Revolutionary Science" and the Terror of International Imperialism, of Colonialism and Neo-Colonialism,
President Ahmed Sékou Touré.

Table 1. Estimated Agricultural Production, Selected Years (in thousands of metric tons)*

| Food Crops | 1964 | 1965 | 1968 | 1969 | 1970 | 1971 | 1972 | 1973[a] | 1974[a] |
|---|---|---|---|---|---|---|---|---|---|
| Rice (paddy) | 360 | 300 | 250 | 270 | 240 | 220 | 200 | 300 | 400[b] |
| Cassava | 420 | 390 | 370 | 350 | 270 | 250 | 220 | - | - |
| Millets, sorghum, fonio | 146 | 150 | 150 | 150 | 130 | 120 | 90 | - | - |
| Sweet potatoes | 85 | 73 | 80 | 82 | 70 | 50 | 30 | - | - |
| Maize (corn) | 70 | 73 | 68 | 68 | 52 | 50 | 48 | 260[b] | 300[b] |
| | | | | | | | | | |
| Export Crops | | | | | | | | | |
| Bananas | 40 | 37 | 35 | 27 | 30 | 25 | 31 | - | - |
| Pineapples | 16 | 13 | 15 | 25 | 27 | 30 | 33 | - | - |
| Palm kernels | 23 | 25 | 25 | 28 | 30 | 30 | 30 | 40 | 35[c] |
| Coffee (robusta) | 13 | 7 | 15 | 17 | 10 | 9 | 7 | 6.9[c] | 7.5[c] |
| Groundnuts (peanuts) | 18 | 15 | 19 | 18 | 20 | 22 | 25 | 26[b] | 27[b] |
| Citrus fruit | 10 | 6 | 7 | 9 | 4 | 3 | 4 | - | - |

Source: Harold D. Nelson, Area Handbook for Guinea, 2nd ed., Washington, D.C.: U.S. Gov. Printing Office, 1975.

*Statistical information about Guinea can be accepted only with reservation and close analysis since there is a Guinean law against divulging such information. Furthermore, proponents and opponents of the present government often are politically motivated in their presentation of what little information does trickle out of the country. Guinea's reporting year ends September 30.

aSource: United Nations Statistical Yearbook, 1975
bUnited Nations Food and Agriculture Organization estimate
cprovisional, may be unreliable data

Table 2.  Estimated Mining Production, Selected Years

| | 1965 | 1966 | 1967 | 1968 | 1969 | 1970 | 1971 | 1972 | 1973 | 1974 |
|---|---|---|---|---|---|---|---|---|---|---|
| (thousand metric tons) | | | | | | | | | | |
| Iron ore (Fe content) | 378 | 305 | 356 | 935 | 1040 | 1040 | - | - | - | - |
| Bauxite | 1870 | 1609 | 1639 | 2118 | 2459 | 2490 | 2630 | 2650 | 3660 | 6600 |
| (thousand metric carats) | | | | | | | | | | |
| Diamonds, industrial | 51 | 51 | 31 | 49 | 50 | 52 | 52 | 55 | 55 | 55 |
| Diamonds, gem | 21 | 21 | 20 | 21 | 22 | 22 | 22 | 25 | 25 | 25 |

Source:  United Nations Statistical Yearbook, 1975.

# THE DICTIONARY

ADMINISTRATIVE ORGANIZATION. Guinea is a one-party
state in which party and government are, for all practical purposes, one. Major governmental functions are
highly centralized in the hands of the executive and his
appointed cabinet. In effect the President, as head of
state and leader of the only legal party, the PDG or
Parti Démocratique de Guinée (q.v.), dominates all
branches of government. Re-elected in January 1975
for his third seven-year term, President Sékou Touré
appoints his own cabinet, all officials in public administration and all military officers. He drafts almost
all laws and rules, largely by executive decree or administrative fiat. Since 99.8 per cent of the 2.4 million registered voters elected Sékou Touré unanimously
in the 1975 election, this overcentralized executive of-
fice--responsible for the execution of all laws and sign-
ing all government acts--represents the sole source of
all political power. With his prime minister and five
Party leaders the President runs a direct chain of command through every level of administration.

The cabinet has varied from seven to 34 ministers and changes are constantly being made in the
form and function of the ministries. In 1972 this
basic system was reorganized with the creation of two
distinct levels of ministry and an office of prime minister. The government was divided into seven domains
presided over by "super-ministers" who dealt with all
ministries and agencies concerned with some broad
range of national interests. Originally one of these
domains was headed by the president, a second by the
prime minister and the other five by the other members of PDG's Bureau Politique National (q.v.), or
BPN. Sékou Touré's brother, Ismael Touré, for example, was put in charge of the Economy and Finance
Domain, which included the ministries of Industry and
Power, Finance, Banking, Mining and Geology and Public Works, Town Planning and Housing.

1

In practice it is useless to carefully chart an
administrative hierarchy or organization structure be-
cause changes are made at will by the President.  The
PDG, the BPN and the Government of Guinea are ul-
timately no more than extensions of the will of the
"Helmsman of the Guinean Revolution," Ahmed Sékou
Touré.  See LOCAL ADMINISTRATION; REGIONAL AD-
MINISTRATION; ARRONDISSEMENT; LEGAL SYSTEM.

AFRIQUE OCCIDENTALE FRANÇAISE (AOF).   French West
Africa.   One of France's two colonial African federa-
tions, the AOF encompassed the territories of Ivory
Coast, Niger, Upper Volta, Mauritania, Senegal, French
Soudan, Dahomey and Guinea.   Established between 1895
and 1904 with a number of organizational changes over
the years this federation was the largest unit in the
French colonial organization.   In the post-World War II
era the AOF was headed by a governor general in Dakar, Senegal, under the direct control of the Ministry
of Colonies in Paris.   The governor general was as-
sisted by a Conseil de Gouvernement composed of five
delegates from each territory with only consultative
powers.   Each colony had its own governor, responsible to Dakar, and a territorial assembly with severely
limited deliberative authority.   The AOF officially
ceased to exist January 21, 1959.

AGENCE GUINEENNE DE PRESSE (AGP).   The Guinean Press
Agency was a government information service supplying
daily news releases to government officials and the
foreign diplomatic corps.   Its functions have largely
been allowed to lapse in recent years as other government organs supplanted it.   See also HOROYA; JOUR-
NAL OFFICIEL DE LA REPUBLIQUE DE GUINEE.

AGENCE GUINEENNE DE SPECTACLES.   Founded by the
government of Guinea in May 1973 to replace the previous civil society, Syliart.   This government institution
under the Ministry of Youth, Art and Sports provides
support for Guinean artists, authors and playwrights as
well as pensions for retired artists whose works are
in accordance with PDG views.   See SYLIART.

AGRICULTURAL PRODUCTION.   Although Guinea is largely
an agricultural nation, its exports in this sector fell
off considerably in the mid-sixties.   It has become apparent that the government's experimentation with large-

scale cooperative production are not efficient with present management.  The relatively low price paid by the
government to producers coupled with the high prices
and unavailability of consumer goods has caused many
producers to revert to subsistence agriculture and/or
resort to smuggling in order to maintain profits.  Coffee production for export, for example, fell from
11,000 metric tons in 1958 to 7,000 in 1965 and has
declined even further since.  Rice production has declined each year since independence and the goal of
self-sufficiency seems further away than ever today.
The output of the country's other main agricultural
crops including bananas, palm-kernels, peanuts and
citrus fruits has generally declined or grown very
slowly in the past ten years.  (The exception is pineapples which has doubled in production.)  Lack of technical expertise, equipment and capital development expenditures would all seem to represent roadblocks to
the expansion of Guinean agricultural production.  See
Table 1.

AIR GUINEA.  Founded in 1960 this semi-government agency
has operated an irregular service of domestic flights
from Conakry to laterite surface landing strips at
Labê, Bokê, Kankan, Kissidougou, Nzêrêkorê, Siguiri,
Macenta and Gaoual.  Occasional flights to neighboring
capitals as well as government flights for officials,
student groups and Mecca-bound pilgrims are also made.
Soviet-supplied aircraft and foreign as well as Guinean
pilots and technicians continue a very diminished service at present.  See AVIATION.

ALFAYA.  After the death of the successful jihad (q.v.)
leader, Ibrahim Musa (q.v.), in the mid-18th century
Futa Jalon, rival factions developed.  The party which
favored the clerical supporters of the family of Ibrahim Musa were called Alfaya and contended with the
military group, the Soriya (q.v.), who supported the
war leader Ibrahim Sori (q.v.).  These two groups
contended for the position of almany (q.v.) in the Futa
Jalon well into the 20th century.

ALFA YAYA.  A Fulbê traditional leader in Labê, a province
of Futa Jalon, who collaborated with the French conquest in order to achieve his own independence from
the almany (q.v.) of the Futa.  When the French policy
changed he was deported to Dahomey in 1905.  Upon

his return at the end of his exile in 1911 he was accused by the French administration of attempting to re-
trieve his "slaves. " He was then deported to Port
Etienne in 1911 where he died. The current government
of Guinea casts Alfa Yaya as a heroic victim of French
imperialism conveniently ignoring his earlier support of
the French colonial occupation of the Futa Jalon.

AL HAJJ (literally, the pilgrim). Title of respect taken by
any Muslim who has completed the recommended pilgrimage to Mecca. (Also spelled Alhadji, El Hajj, El
Hadj, etc.).

AL HAJJ UMAR. A Fulbé-speaking leader who established a
short-lived Muslim kingdom in the mid-19th century in
what is today Upper Guinea, Eastern Senegal and Western Mali. Born in 1794 he made the pilgrimage to
Mecca about 1826. Returning to West Africa he established a Tijaniyya retreat near Jugunko in the Futa
Jalon. From there he began to develop a group of
followers and in 1852 he declared a jihad against his
enemies in the Futa Toro. Repulsed there and by the
French in 1857 he then overran the "Bambara" kingdom
of Ségou in 1861. Ultimately he carved out a Tijaniyya
state between the Niger and Senegal Rivers which included Timbuktu and the Qadiriyya Muslim state of
Macina. After Al-Hajj Umar was killed in 1864, his
son Ahmad lost to increasing French pressure and
Qadiriyya revolts. See also JIHAD; QADIRIYYA;
TIJANIYYA.

ALMANY. Traditionally the spiritual leader in West African
Muslim societies. An almany was concerned with
prayer, education, and general religious rule-making.
The term gradually came to be applied to some secular
as well as religious leaders in Guinea. A notable
almany was Samory Touré (q. v.).

ALUMINA. This aluminum oxide produced from bauxite is,
along with the raw ore bauxite, Guinea's major export.
Produced by foreign investors, alumina and bauxite are
the major foreign exchange sources for the government
of Guinea with over 800,000 metric tons of alumina
produced yearly in recent years. At present Guinea
has not harnessed its hydroelectrical potential to the
production of aluminum and world market supplies of
alumina and bauxite are such that the Guinean portion

of the market is still negligible, but it is growing.

AMARIA.  A small village on the Konkouré River upstream
from the alumina plant and bauxite mines of Fria.  A
720,000-kilowatt hydroelectric plant was planned here
in the Five Year Development Plan of 1973-1978.

ANGLO-FRENCH CONVENTION OF 1882.  By terms of the
British Foreign Office this agreement granted most
French claims along the coast between Conakry and
Freetown.  This convention was never officially ratified
by the French Chamber of Deputies.  It was, though,
typical of European diplomatic activities of the 19th
century which largely established today's national boundaries, but paid little or no heed to African realities.

ANIMAL HUSBANDRY.  Guinea was a livestock exporter before independence but by the mid 1960s the flight of
many Guinean herders to the Ivory Coast, Liberia and
Sierra Leone had made meat a very rare item in the
diets of most Guineans.  Scrawny chickens are found
throughout the country along with an occasional duck
and a rare turkey or Guinea fowl, but few of these
animals are ever marketed.  They are usually kept
as a ready source of meat for the occasional village
festival or honored guest.  A few pigs are kept in the
forest region where fewer Muslims live.  N'dana
cattle, small, agile and strong with good resistance to
disease, especially the tsetse fly (q.v.), which carries
sleeping sickness, are allowed to wander and graze
almost at will throughout much of Upper Guinea and the
Futa Jalon.  Small short-haired sheep and goats also
exist in relatively large numbers throughout Guinea.
          Dry season hunger keeps all of these animals
from ever becoming very productive.  Unselective
breeding and the forced sale of animals by government
requisition also militates against the creation of higher
milk or meat yields at present.

ARMED FORCES.  Under the constitution, the president of
the Republic is the commander-in-chief of the armed
forces.  Since 1972 the minister of the people's army
has been under the domain of the prime minister with
Namary Keita as chief of staff.  Distrusted by Sékou
Touré, the armed forces have never played a very large
role in Guinean affairs and have been somewhat over-
shadowed by the Militia (Milices Populaires q.v.),  the

Gendarmerie (q. v. ), Sûreté Nationale (q. v. ) and Garde
Républicaine (q. v. ).  The Army has fewer than 5000
officers and its personnel are organized into four infan-
try battalions, one armored battalion and one engineer
battalion.  Little information is available about the Air
Force, with perhaps 300 members, and the Navy, with
about 200 officers and personnel.  Defense spending
ranges from about 4 or 5 per cent of the Guinean GNP
to as much as 11. 5 per cent but the armed forces are
often mobilized for developmental activities in agriculture and road building, so defense costs are perhaps
not this high.

ARRONDISSEMENT.  The administrative level between the
regional and local levels.  There were 220 such districts
in 1974.  Each arrondissement was presided over by
an executive head called a commandant who was responsible to the governor of the region.  Within the
arrondissement party structures exactly paralleled
those of the government.  The arrondissement had
been the basic administrative unit of the French colonial
government in West Africa and the lowest over which a
French officer presided directly.  See ADMINISTRATIVE
ORGANIZATION.

ASSIMILATION POLICY.  In theory this was the policy of
French colonial administration in Africa.  It supposedly
assumed that Africans would eventually become black
French.  Only 2000 Africans in the A. O. F. (q. v. )
were ever able to meet the French language, dress,
education, religion, and other requirements and overcome the complex petition requirements to obtain French
citizenship and thus escape the corvée (q. v. ) and
indigénat (q. v. ).  See ASSOCIATION POLICY.

ASSIMILE.  Name given to those few Africans who, within
the French colonial system, met a whole range of
educational, economic and social standards--in effect
adopted the French way of life, and were thus, in
theory, to be granted the full privileges of French
citizenship.  Until 1946 when reforms made French
citizenship more readily available, only a handful of
Guineans sought or received this status.

ASSOCIATION DES GUINEENS EN FRANCE (AGF).  One of
the two opposition groups in exile from Guinea.  Like
its counterpart, the Front pour la Libération Nationale

de Guinêe (q. v.), it is composed largely of university
graduates and Guinean veterans of the French military.
These groups also number former cabinet ministers
and former Guinean ambassadors among their members.

ASSOCIATION INTER-GOUVERNEMENTALE DES PAYS
   PRODUCTEURS DE BAUXITE (IBA).  Association of
   Bauxite-producing countries formed in March 1974.
   Members are Guinea, Sierra Leone, Guyana, Jamaica,
   Yugoslavia, Surinam, and Australia.

ASSOCIATION POLICY.  The colonial policy which by the
   1920's had, in practice, replaced earlier theoretical
   attempts to assimilate Africans into the French culture.
   Under this policy Africans were considered to be incapable of becoming French in the near future so they
   were "allowed" to retain their manners, customs and
   religion while political and economic control was in
   French hands.  See ASSIMILATION POLICY.

AVIATION.  Guinea's internal air service, Air Guinêe (q. v.),
   is run as a public enterprise.  It had lost over $3
   million by the early seventies and showed no sign of
   becoming self-supporting.  The Conakry-Gbessia airport (q. v.) can take aircraft of the Boeing 707 size
   while two other regional airports can take medium-
   range aircraft and offer night landing facilities.  Six
   other small unsurfaced, laterite strips are servicable
   for daylight and dry season use by smaller aircraft.


                          -B-


BADIARANKE (Badyarankê).  An ethnic group closely related
   to the Conaigui (q. v.) and Bassari (q. v.) living on the
   Senegal-Guinea border.  Beekeepers and farmers, they
   raised few cows but were once well known as cotton
   cloth weavers.  Little assimilated into national life
   until relatively recently, they have maintained a larger
   degree of cultural and religious autonomy than most of
   Guinea's ethnic groups.

BAFING RIVER.  The upper course of the Senegal River
   having its source less than 50 kilometers north of
   Mamou in the south-central Futa Jalon.  From its
   source it flows north and northeast to the border of
   Mali and from there to the sea as the Senegal River.

BAGA.   The largest of the minor ethnic groups in Lower
Guinea.   Predating the later Susu populations in the
coastal areas from Conakry to the Rio Núñez estuary
they were present on the coast from at least the 16th
century.   Largely assimilated into the dominant Susu
populations of Lower Guinea by the early 1970s.   See
LANDOUMA.

BAKOYE RIVER.   An important tributary of the Senegal
River taking its rise just inside the Guinea border to
the north of Siguiri in the ancient gold mining area of
Bouré.   See BOURE.

BALAFON.   The Maninka name for a wooden xylophone widely
played in traditional orchestras throughout Guinea and
elsewhere in West Africa.

BALLET AFRICAIN.   Founded by Fodéba Keita in the 1950s,
this troupe displayed traditional West African art to the
world.   It was originally composed of singers, dancers
and instrumentalists from various parts of French West
Africa.   Constituted as a Guinean national ballet troop
in 1959 it receives government support and performs
throughout Europe and America.

BANANAS (Musa sapientum spp.).   Representing an important
export crop in Guinea, this large herbaceous perennial
plant growing from 3 to 9 meters high is best grown
under irrigation in the relatively sheltered well-drained
and fertile areas.

BANKING.   With the central bank under direct executive
control by the President, banking functions in Guinea
largely consist of maintaining credit and support functions for government agencies and state enterprises.
Individual deposits and withdrawals in savings are very
rare and credit to the private sector consists of less
than 5 per cent of total credit.

BANQUE CENTRALE DE LA REPUBLIQUE DE GUINEE (BCRG).
Established on March 1, 1960, it operated, in principle,
as a semi-autonomous institution, issuing currency,
regulating the volume of credit, acting as banker for the
government, and participating in the formulation of
monetary and fiscal policies.   In 1972 President Touré
took over as governor of the bank and attached it
directly to the Presidency; since then its previously

limited freedom from executive control has been totally
lost.

BANQUE CENTRALE DES ETATS DE L'AFRIQUE DE
L'OUEST (BCEAO).
French West Africa's central bank, established in Paris
in 1958 with branches in all members states.   Guinea's
decision on March 1, 1960, to create an independent
currency removed Guinea from participation in this bank.

BANQUE GUINEENNE DE COMMERCE EXTERIEUR (BGCE).
One of three specialized banks developed in 1961 after
four of five French private commercial banks had their
licenses revoked in August 1960.   The Guinean Bank
for Foreign Trade, like the other specialized banks,
bases its credit expansion partly upon deposits made
with them and partly upon borrowing from the central
bank.

BANQUE NATIONALE POUR LE DEVELOPPEMENT AGRICOLE
(BNDA).   One of the three specialized banks developed
in 1961 after four of five French private commercial
banks had their licenses revoked in August 1960.   The
National Bank for Agricultural Development made possible the acquisition of tractors on easy terms by private entrepreneurs for a time, but credit to small-
holders, which was extended by the cooperative system,
has been severely limited since 1964.

BAOBAB (Adansonia digitata).   A common savanna and grassland tree with a short, wide trunk.   It bears an edible
fruit, the seed of which can also be eaten roasted.   The
leaves serve as green vegetables and animal fodder.
Because of the relative scarcity of trees on the savanna
and the tree's striking appearance it came to be associated with magical phenomena among many Guinean
peoples.

BARRY III   see BARRY, IBRAHIMA

BARRY, DIAWADOU.   A son of the Almany of Dabola,   this
Fulbé political leader from the Futa Jalon represented
the traditional "chiefs" and most white residents of the
Futa Jalon in the mid-1954 election for the delegate to the
French National Assembly from Guinea.   Barry was
declared elected in an election rife with irregularities
by the French Colonial Government in spite of the fact

that Sékou Touré probably gained the majority of votes
throughout most of Guinea.  With the decline of traditional Fulbé authority in the late 1950s Barry's power
waned.  Arrested in 1965 as an opponent of the PDG,
Barry played no further rule in Guinean politics.

BARRY, IBRAHIMA (BARRY III).  Born of Fulbé peasants
at Bantigrel in the Pita district he studied at William
Ponty School and utimately qualified as a lawyer in
France.  He ran for the post of deputy in the French
National Assembly in 1954 and 1956 but was defeated
on both occasions.  As secretary general of the Mouvement Socialiste Africain and then as secretary general
of a short lived Union Populaire de Guinée he opposed
Sékou Touré.  He reconciled these differences in 1958
and served in cabinet posts through the mid 1960s.
In 1971 he was hanged in Conakry allegedly for treason.

BASSARI.  This is one of the least Europeanized or Islami-
cized ethnic groups in Guinea.  Historically among the
oldest inhabitants of Guinea the Bassari preserve their
traditional matrilineal organization, religion and way of
life in the rugged areas of the Futa Jalon close to the
Guinea-Bissau and Senegal borders.

BAUXITE.  Guinea has several major deposits of this aluminum producing ore.  These are chiefly located in the
Futa Jalon and its foothills since the deposits which
existed in the Iles de Los had practically been ex-
hausted by 1972.  Guinea has 3. 5 billion tons of known
reserves.  World supplies are estimated at somewhat
less than 16 billion tons.  So Guinea ought to become
a major world exporter of bauxite by the mid 1970s.

BEAVOGUI, LOUIS LANSANA.  Born in Macenta in 1923, he
was trained as a medic in Dakar.  At the age of 31
he was elected mayor of Kissidougou.  In January
1956 he, along with Sékou Touré and Saifoulaye Diallo,
was elected to the French National Assembly from
Guinea.  Upon independence he was made minister
for economic affairs and planning.  In 1961 he became
minister of foreign affairs, an office he held for almost
eight years.  He was active in the United Nations
debate on the Congo in 1965.  In October 1966, while
en route to the OAU conference in Addis Ababba, he
was held by Ghanaian officials at the Accra airport in
retaliation for the refuge Guinea had offered to the

exiled Kwame Nkrumah. In May 1969 he replaced Ismael
Touré as minister of economic affairs.

On April 26, 1972, at the closing session of the
Ninth Congress of the PDG, President Touré announced
that Beavogui was to fill the newly created post of
prime minister.  He was also placed in charge of the
Army, Foreign Affairs, Planning, Financial Control
and Information.  Two months later Foreign Affairs was
given to Fily Cissoko but it remains apparent that
President Touré trusts the dedicated and hardworking
Beavogui very much.

BEHANZIN, SENAINDOU.  Born in Dahomey, Behanzin has
played an important role in the educational policies of
Guinea since independence.  Closely associated with
Sékou Touré, Behanzin is one of the most trusted of
Touré cabinet members.

BENTY.  Once a relatively important trading town on the
Mélikouré River south of Conakry.  This small port
was still active in banana exporting until the late
1960s but by the mid-seventies the small coastal
transport lighters which served this and other small
ports had ceased operation and Benty has declined
in importance.

BEYLA.  A town and administrative region of the same name
in the northeast forest region on the Ivory Coast border.
Beyla was the center of a thriving tobacco growing
area until independence.  Though the Beyla region is
also on the edge of a major diamond mining area it
remains a scarcely populated subsistence agricultural
area for the most part.

BILHARZIA (Schistosomiasis).  A common infectious disease
in Guinea caused by a parasite blood fluke which requires
a tiny fresh water snail as an intermediate vector.
People are infected by walking in, swimming or drink-
ing water containing the larvae of the fluke.  Since
prevention and treatment are difficult many Guineans
suffer from this disease to varying degrees.

BISSANDOUGOU.  The capital of the short lived Maninka
state established by Samory Touré in the late 19th
century near present day Kérouané (q. v. ) in the north
of the Forest Region.  See TOURE, SAMORY.

BLOC AFRICAIN DE GUINEE (BAG).  A political party
    founded in 1954 by Barry Diawadou and Keita Kouman-
    dian to unite various rump groups of regional parties
    against the growing power of Sékou Touré's Parti
    Démocratique de Guinée (PDG).  Briefly called the
    Union Progressiste de Guinée in 1958 it merged in
    the same year with PDG.

BOFFA.  A town and region north of Conakry on the Atlantic
    coast which was an early site of European trade and
    colonial penetration.  Largely a subsistence agricul-
    tural area in the 20th century, its rice producing
    possibilities and potential as a port for bauxite and
    alumina exports may again give it importance in the
    future.

BOKE.  A town and region located at the Atlantic coast near
    the border with Guinea-Bissau.  Established as a French
    garrison in 1866, today the Boké region is the center of
    the thriving bauxite mining industry with a new railway
    and port facilities.  The bauxite in the region has a
    60 per cent aluminum content with a very low silica
    content, making this perhaps 200-million ton deposit
    one of the highest grade bauxite deposits in the world.

BOKE PROJECT.  The most important, and to date, most
    successful of the industrial units established since
    independence.  This bauxite mining project was started
    in 1973 under the authority of a joint stock company
    owned 49 percent by the government of Guinea and 51
    per cent by a consortium of Western aluminium companies.
    The project is expected ultimately to produce $50
    million a year for the Guinean treasury and make
    Guinea one of the world's major bauxite producers.
    See COMPAGNIE DES BAUXITES DE GUINEE.

BORDO.  A village outside of Kankan, the second largest
    city in Guinea, where the French established an arts
    and trade school.  The school had an agricultural
    experimental station connected to it which largely
    ceased functioning after independence.

BOUBOU.  The traditional, simple flowing robe worn by all
    but the very poorest men on public and ceremonial
    occasions.  Well dressed women might also wear a
    voluminous transparent gauze boubou over a skirt,
    fashioned from a piece of cloth tied around the waist,
    and a blouse of like color.

BRAZZAVILLE CONFERENCE. A meeting called by the Free
French under General de Gaulle in January 1944 and
presided over by the Commissioners for the Colonies in
the French National Liberation Committee. This gather-
ing of French colonial governors and administrators,
parliamentarians and non-Communist labor leaders
reiterated their support of the colonial system though
they promised to lessen the harshest aspects of colonial
"native policy" after the war.

BRIGADES DE PRODUCTION. These work groups are a
continuation of the investissement humain of the early
years of independence in Guinea. Putting into practice
the principle produire pour se suffire, groups from all
sectors of the Guinean population, including the army
and students, are drafted into production brigades.
Brigades are of two types: those in which all production plans are directed by the government and the
government supplies all the equipment, and those in
which local communities make the decisions. The
1973-1978 five year plan called for 2000 brigades in
1974, 3000 in 1975, 4500 in 1976, 5500 in 1977 and
7125 in 1978.

BURE (Bourê). The ancient alluvial gold field north of present day Siguiri. This gold field was an important
source of wealth for the ancient Mali Empire but is
now largely worked out.

BUREAU POLITIQUE NATIONAL (BPN). National Political
Bureau. The seven-member central committee of the
Parti Démocratique de Guinée (PDG--q. v.). Made up
of the president, prime minister, and five other Party
leaders, this group controls the government, appoints
about one third of the National Assembly and directs,
through the Party, control of all authorized political
activity within the country.

-C-

CABRAL, AMILCAR (1926-1973). The founder in 1956 of
the Partido Africâo da Independência da Guidê e do
Cabo-Verde (PAIGC--q. v. ), which in 1963 launched the
war for independence from Portugual of Guinea-Bissau.
Cabral was assassinated in Conakry in 1973 where the
PAIGC had its headquarters.

CAILLE, RENE-AUGUSTE (1799-1838). A European who traveled through a part of Upper Guinea to Timbuktu in
1824-1828. His accounts of this journey, published in
1830, whetted the European appetite for further exploration and ultimately conquest of West Africa.

CAISSE NATIONALE D'EPARGNE (CNE). The National Savings Bank is, along with a postal checking system, a
government-run agency with no real credit function.

CAMARA, LAYE. A Maninka from Kouroussa, Camara Laye
is the best-known Guinean author. His L'Enfant noir
(The Black Child) appeared in 1953 and was followed by
Le Regard du roi (in 1954) and Dramouss (in 1966).
This last novel, which appeared in France, depicts an
African country under the control of a tyrannical dic-
tator. Camara Laye now lives in exile in Senegal.

CANTON. A group of villages placed under an indigenous
administrative agent or chief who was responsible to the
Commandant de Cercle (q. v. ) during the French colonial
regime. See CHIEFTANCY.

CATHOLIC MISSIONS. The first French Catholic mission was
established in Boffa in 1877 and by 1967 about 26,000
Guineans were Catholic. The White Fathers and the
Holy Ghost Fathers were the major Catholic missionary
groups active in Guinea throughout the colonial period
when the military and colonial occupation of Guinea was
paralleled by mission activities. White priests with
their beards and soutanes were widely known throughout
Guinea by the 1920s. Installed in small chapels throughout the country they soon established elementary schools
and dispensaries. But in general, the paternalistic
attitude, the lack of schools of higher learning and the
inability to adjust to the changes brought about by independence, along with a certain de-Africanization which
seemed to characterize African Catholics have led to a
diminishing of Catholic influence in Guinea. In 1967
white missionaries were expelled from Guinea and in
1970 the African-born archbishop of Conakry, Raymond
Tchidimbo (q. v. ) was condemned to life in prison.

CENTRE DE MODERNISATION RURALE (CMR). According to
the first Three Year Plan, these Centers of Rural Mod-
ernization were to be established in each administrative
region. They were to serve as model enterprises for

the training of local farmers, the demonstration of new
materials and the propagation of modern methods. Within three years of their creation in 1960 the CMRs were
in ruins. Their property, especially the tractors, was
taken over for private use by officials. Their failure
was due to inadequate finance and mismanagement.

CENTRE D'EDUCATION REVOLUTIONNAIRE (CER). A term
now generally used as a synonym for "school" in Guinea.
This change in terminology was based on the change of
educational concepts in the late 1960s which provided
that all schools would be transformed into institutions
providing for work-study programs which combine production with education. See EDUCATION.

CENTRE NATIONAL DE PRODUCTION AGRICOLE (CNPA).
State farms which were to be organized under the first
Three Year Plan. Some of these were to be models
of highly mechanized farming. But by mid 1963 none
of the 20 CNPAs planned had been fully established and
most were gradually abandoned in the next few years.

CERCLE. The basic unit of French colonial territorial administration directly controlled by the French. Each
such area was headed by a district commandant, a
civil official with extensive powers, who was directly
responsible to the governor.

CFA FRANC. Originally the Colonies Françaises d'Afrique
franc, the name was changed in 1962 to Communauté
Financière Africaine. This is the freely transferable
currency of most of the former territories of the former French West Africa and French Equatorial Africa
except for Guinea (and Mali for a period) but with the
addition of Tunisia, Togo and Cameroon. This currency is pegged to the French franc into which it is freely
convertible. The central bank since 1974 has been located in Dakar, Senegal. See CURRENCY.

CHERIF, SEKOU. One of the few younger cabinet members
in the 1970s. Cherif is a well-educated, hard-working
and effective administrator. His efficient functioning
as minister for local development for Middle Guinea
may well be the beginning of more professional and
effective management in years to come.

CHIEFTANCY. The process by which French colonial ad-

ministration in Guinea functioned at the lowest level.
Placed by the lieutenant governor on the recommendation
of the commandant de cercle (q. v. ) the "chief" was an
African administrative agent over a canton, or group of
villages.   He was called upon to obey every command
given to him from above.    Forced to live upon a mea-
ger allowance from taxes they collected, the "chiefs"
were open to a great deal of corruption and were almost
universally despised by Guineans.

CHINA.   In 1960 the People's Republic of China began their
aid program to Africa with an interest-free loan equivalent to  US $25 million  given to President Touré
while he was on a state visit to Peking.   Curtailed somewhat in the  mid  1960s PRC aid has continued to be an
important source of development help.    By 1970 China
was Guinea's third largest source of imports.    Guinea
depends heavily on Chinese rice to meet continued food
shortages.

CISSE, EMILE.   A Guinean writer whose publications in the
1950s dealt with the independence struggle.

COCOLI   see  LANDOUMA

COFFEE (Coffea robusta).    Long an important export crop
of the Forest Region, coffee in Guinea faces a number
of severe production problems.    The coffees grown in
Guinea are all robusta varieties which were long a surplus commodity on the world market.    Cultivated in
small holdings or inefficiently managed collective fields,
Guinean coffee has suffered from recurrent onslaughts
of disease.    With government prices fixed far too low
perhaps as much as 50 per cent of the crop has been
smuggled out of the country through Liberia and Sierra
Leone.

COMITE  CENTRAL (Central Committee).    Since early 1975
this highest organ of the PDG (q. v. ) has been the policy
making and guidance body of the Party, responsible for
directing and controlling the country's political, economic,
social,  cultural and administrative affairs through its
executive agent the Bureau Politique National (q. v. ),
which is chaired by President Touré.    Along with the
BPN, the Central Committee is composed of 12 other
cabinet ministers, the party's permanent secretary and
four other appointed members.

**COMITE D'UNITE DE PRODUCTION (CUP).** Committees of
production which were supposed to be set up within administrative services and public enterprises so that
workers could participate in the preparation and imple-
mentation of the production plan. Worker participation
in budget formation and operation of the enterprise was
to be assured by these committees. By 1971, President
Touré himself admitted that the CUPs had never really
performed their function.

**COMITE NATIONAL DES FEMMES (CNF).** Organized as an
auxiliary to the PDG, the CNF has played an important
part in the social and political affairs of Guinea. This
organization is a pressure group within the Party which
watches over women's affairs. Cutting across ethnic,
religious and linguistic divisions, this single national
women's organization has helped unite the country and
establish women on an equal footing with men in many
important aspects of political activity.

**COMMANDANT DE CERCLE.** A French official under the
colonial regime in Guinea who directly ruled over and
appointed African canton chiefs. Most present-day regions
in Guinea reflect these French administrative cercles.

**COMMUNAUTE FRANÇAISE.** The "free" association of autonomous republics set up when the French Constitution
of the Fifth Republic was ratified in 1954 by most of
the French colonies in Africa. The only exception was
Guinea, which opted for independence. In 1960 these
associated republics attained jurisdiction over their own
foreign policy, defense, currency and fiscal matters,
and external communications through an amendment to
the French constitution.

**COMPAGNIE DE BAUXITE DE GUINEE (CBG--Bauxite Com-
pany of Guinea).** A mixed enterprise in which the government of Guinea held 49 per cent of the shares and
took 65 per cent of any net profits in taxes. The company operated the Boké (q. v.) Bauxite mines with HALCO
(q. v.), a consortium of Alcan, Martin Marietta, Pechiney-
Ugine-Kuhlmann, the Vereinigte Aluminium Werke and
Montecatini-Elison. See BOKE PROJECT.

**COMPAGNIE FRANÇAISE DE L'AFRIQUE OCCIDENTALE
(CFAO).** One of a number of foreign firms which dominated commercial life in Guinea during colonial times.

These firms controlled the import-export and wholesale
trade and some aspects of retail trade until state controlled enterprise severely curtailed their operations
after independence.

COMPTOIR GUINEEN DU COMMERCE EXTERIEUR (CGCE).
A state enterprise founded in January 1959 to handle
Guinea's trade relations with the Eastern Bloc countries
which had tied up much of Guinea's export production
in a variety of aid-trade agreements.  The CGCE was
granted a full monopoly over rice, sugar and cement
imports along with a partial monopoly over banana, palm
products and coffee exports.  The comptoir was abolished
in September 1961 because of its total inability to handle
the job.

COMPTOIR GUINEEN DU COMMERCE INTERIEUR (CGCI).
A state enterprise founded in May 1960 with a full monopoly over the wholesale trade throughout the country.  Regional comptoirs were established in the headquarters
of each administrative region to serve as subsidaries of
the CGCI.  Retail trade was left in private hands.  The
CGCI was abolished in September 1961 and a number of
national commercial enterprises were established to replace this poorly managed internal trade monopoly.

CONAKRY.  This city is the capital of Guinea and the major
urban center in the country.  It has somewhat less than
200,000 inhabitants.  Stretching from the old colonial
city on Timbo Island some 35 km. inland on the Kaloum
Peninsula, this city with its urbanized industrial zone
forms the only large scale modernized area of Guinea.

CONAKRY-GBESSIA AIRPORT.  An international airport on
the Kaloum penninsula adjacent to Conakry.  It is served
by scheduled flights of six international airlines, including Air Afrique and the national airline of the USSR,
Czechoslovakia and the German Democratic Republic.
The landing facilities can take aircraft of the Boeing
707 size.  See also AVIATION.

CONFEDERATION GENERAL DU TRAVAIL (CGT).  This General Confederation of Labor was one of the earliest labor unions in French West Africa;  it was modeled on
French communist labor confederations.  As leaders of
this union's Guinean branch, Sékou Touré and his closest
associates first gained their mass following.  By 1953

the CGT had 2,600 members, which Touré led in a
strike for higher wages.  Success in this effort led to
an increase in union membership to 39,000 by 1955 and
finally to Touré's election to the Territorial Assembly
from Guinea.  See LABOR UNIONS;  UNION GENERALE
DES TRAVAILLEURS....

CONFEDERATION NATIONALE DES TRAVAILLEURS DE
      GUINEE (CNTG)  see  LABOR UNIONS; UNION GENERALE
      DES TRAVAILLEURS ...

CONIAGUI.  One of a number of minor ethnic groups living
      around Koundara in the northern part of Middle Guinea
      and over into Guinea-Bissau.  Apparently one of the
      original inhabitants of the area, they have been pushed
      into small pockets by dominant Maninka and Fulbé
      groups in the past 500 years.

CONSEIL ECONOMIQUE NATIONAL.  Council established by
      President Touré in June 1974 to oversee international
      agreements, exports and imports, domestic industries,
      development programs, prices and salaries.

CONSEIL NATIONAL DE LA REVOLUTION (CNR).  This is
      the representative body of the PDG (q. v.) which in
      Guinea is particularly synonymous with government.
      It is summoned in ordinary session twice a year and
      consists of about 150 delegates from the 30 party feder-
      ations throughout the nation.  It is, in theory, a popular
      advisary body but in practice it has little more than a
      "rubber stamp" function as more and more power is
      assumed by the Office of the President.  See PARTI-
      ETAT.

CONSTITUTION.  The Constitution enacted immediately after
      independence in 1958 is, in theory, still the governing
      document under which Guinea functions today.  In prac-
      tice the constitution has been altered, bent and totally
      ignored as suits the objectives of President Sékou Touré
      and the PDG (q. v.).  Only two amendments have formally
      been added but many laws, regulations and presidential
      decrees, many in direct and obvious conflict with the
      constitution, have altered most of its provisions.  See
      PARTI-ETAT.

COOPERATIVE AGRICOLES DE PRODUCTION (CAP).  Under
      the Three-Year Plan these cooperatives of agricultural

production were to be established to involve farmers in
the collective use of new farming materials and, in
some cases, to lead to the mechanized cultivation of
collective farms. Only 291 of these cooperatives were
formed by 1963, instead of the 500 envisaged in the
plan. By 1965 few CAPs existed. See COOPERATIVES.

COOPERATIVE DE PRODUCTION AGRICOLE ET DE CONSOM-
MATION (COPAC). In 1965 this institution was created
at the regional level to buy agricultural produce from
farmers and sell it to the national export enterprise.
In return it was to buy consumer goods from the national enterprises in charge and sell them to the farmers.
In 1966 the function of supplying consumer goods was
taken away. In 1970 the COPACs were abolished when
it was found that they were not selling rural produce
properly.

COOPERATIVES. Originally established in 1960 in order to
qualify for the credits, services, supplies and rental
tractors supplied by the government through rural mod-
ernization centers in administrative regions, village
producer cooperatives numbered some 492 in 1962 but
never involved more than 4 per cent of the country's
cultivators. By 1964 most cooperatives were inactive.
Revived in 1965 in conjunction with consumer cooperatives the cooperative movement in Guinea faltered because of poor management and lack of government support
as well as lack of mass support.

CORVEE. Forced labor imposed upon Africans for purposes
of public construction and administration by French
colonial officials until 1946 as part of the indigènat
(q. v.). Corvée did not apply to the few Africans who
achieved French citizenship but the vast majority of
Africans were potentially victims of this onerous exact-
ment.

COYAH. An important crossroad of commerce during recent
colonial times, this town is located at the juncture of
the Conakry-Kindia road and the road south to Forê-
cariah and the Sierra Leone border. With no administrative function it has declined in importance since independence.

CREDIT NATIONAL POUR LE COMMERCE, L'INDUSTRIE ET
L'HABITAT. The National Credit Institution for Trade,

Industry and Housing was one of three specialized banks
developed in 1961 after four of five French private commercial banks had their licenses revoked in August 1960.
This bank bases its credit expansion partly upon deposits made with it by government agencies and state enterprises and partly upon borrowing from the central
government.

CURRENCY.  From March 1, 1960, to October 2, 1972, the
Guinean Franc was the official currency of Guinea, replacing the CFA franc (q. v.), which was tied to the
French franc, which had previously been used.  The
official exchange rate of the Guinean Franc from March
1, 1960, through December 31, 1971, was 246.8 Guinean
Francs per US $1.  On October 2, 1972, the Guinean
Syli (GS) consisting of 100 cauris, became the official
currency.  It was officially exchanged at a rate of US
$1 for 22.7 Guinean Sylis from October 2, 1972 through
February 13, 1973; subsequently the rate was GS 20.46
for US $1.  Guinean currency is non-convertible and
clandestine sales often place its value at a fourth or a
fifth of the official rates.


-D-


DABOLA.  A town and region in the Futa Jalon between Mamou
and Kankan on the railway.  Possessing untapped bauxite potential, Dabola remains a charming backwater
town due to the poor roads and railroad service at this
distance from the capital.

DALABA.  A town and region of the Futa Jalon between Labé
and Mamou.  Long an important regional market, Dalaba was also a favorite resort spot for Europeans in
colonial times.  Consequently the town has continued to
produce considerable vegetables and fruits for Guinean
markets.  Once also a center of cattle production, it
has declined in importance in recent years in spite of
attempts at improving the local breeds.

DE GAULLE, CHARLES (1890-1970).  A French political and
military leader who founded the Free French movement
against the Germans in World War II.  Receiving much
support in Africa he called the Brazzaville Conference
(q. v.) in 1944 to announce some political, economic,
and social reforms for the French African colonies.

In 1958 he took over the French government and established a new constitution which was to give the French
colonies limited self-government in a French Community.
This draft constitution sought to create a French Community, with France's overseas possessions being granted some degree of autonomy. In a speech in Conakry
in August 1958, De Gaulle stated that the rejection of
this community in a referendum would cast Guinea out
of the community; dire consequences were implied.
Guinea went on to soundly reject the French community
on September 28, 1958, and thus became an autonomous
republic, much to De Gaulle's displeasure.

DEMOCRATIE SOCIALISTE DE GUINEE (DSG--Socialist Dem-
ocracy of Guinea). An elite-oriented party associated
with the socialist movement in France founded by IBRA-
HIMA BARRY (q. v. ) in 1954. In January 1957 the DSG
had become a member of a Mouvement Socialiste Africain but it never really achieved much power in
Guinea.

DIAKHANKE. A Mandé people whose contributions of learned
Muslim scholars to the Fulbé community enabled them
to form a privileged enclave at Touba in Middle Guinea
near Gaoual until the early part of the 19th century.
Claiming ancient ancestory in the historic Empire of
Ghana their descendants today still represent an urban
and fairly wealthy group.

DIAKHITE, MOUSSA. Born at Diarakourou near Kankan in
1927, he received administrative training in Bamako
In October 1946, at age 19, he took part in the RDA
meetings at Bamako. He served as a civil servant
with the AOF administration until he was elected deputy mayor of Kankan in 1956. In 1957 he was elected
to the Guinea Territorial Assembly. He served in a
number of posts after independence, the latest being
Superminister of the Interior and Security domain.

DIALLO, ABDOULAYE. Born of Fulbé parents in January
1917 at Konsondougou near Dabola, Diallo was educated
at the William Ponty School in Dakar. As a civil servant under the French he became active in the trade
union movement. He first opposed and then joined
Sékou Touré's Union Général des Travailleurs d'Afrique
Noire (q. v. ). Diallo returned to Guinea from the
French Soudan after the referendum of September 1958

and served in a number of governmental positions.   As
of March 1976 he was the minister of labor.

DIALLO, SAIFOULAYE.   Born in 1923 at Diari near Labé,
    Diallo received a normal school education at William
    Ponty School in Dakar.   He served throughout the AOF
    as a civil servant and was frequently moved because of
    his trade union activity.   He was active in RDA affairs
    through AOF and in January 1956 he was elected to the
    French National Assembly.   In March 1957 he was
    elected to the Guinean Territorial Assembly and served
    as its first president.   At independence he was elected
    president of the National Assembly.   In 1963 he was
    appointed minister of state for finance and planning and
    in May 1969 he replaced Beavogui as minister for
    foreign affairs.   Ill health has caused him to be less
    active, and his appointment as minister at the Presi-
    dency in June 1972 was largely honorary, though he
    continued to hold ministerial rank through at least 1976.

DIALLO, YACINE.   A socialist member of the French assem-
    bly from Guinea which adopted the 1946 constitution
    making French Black Africa a part of the French Re-
    public as members of the French Union (q. v. ).   As head of
    the Démocratie Socialiste de Guinée (q. v. ), Diallo re-
    ceived most of his support from the French educated
    elite and with his death in 1954 the party declined in
    strength.

DIALONKE (Djallonké, Dyaloké, Jallonké).   A Mandé popula-
    tion of the south and central part of the Futa Jalon who
    inhabited the Futa before the Fulbé state was established
    in the 18th century.   Accepting Islam and staying on
    as allies of the Fulbé, or fleeing south and east, these
    people are one of many Mandé populations scattered
    through West Africa by events  of the past 500 years.

DIAMONDS.   Guinea produces both gem and industrial dia-
    monds in some quantity.   Alluvial deposits between
    Kissidougou, Beyla and Kérouané produced 643,000 ca-
    rats in 1959 but since independence no reliable statis-
    tics on production are available.   Most sources agree
    that many stones are smuggled out of the country and
    that technical expertise is somewhat lacking.   New
    pipes of kimberlite discovered in the Forécariah ad-
    ministrative region in 1963 and 1964 have as yet failed
    to produce many stones.

**DIANE, LANSANA.** Little is known of General Diané's past
before 1958 though he probably had some post-elemen-
tary school training in animal husbandry. At independence he was appointed governor of Kankan and N'Zérêkoré. In 1960 he was major-general of the Guinean
army and served as the head of the 749-man battalion
sent to the Congo as part of the United Nations peace
force. He was appointed governor of Labé in 1961 and
helped to still persistent resistance to Touré's regime
in that area. He served in a variety of ministerial
positions until November 20, 1970, when Portuguese
and Guinean opponents to Touré's regime captured him
during an attack on Conakry. He apparently escaped
but was thereafter relegated to lesser Party positions
by the President.

**DIECKE FOREST.** A reserve of primary forest in the
N'Zérêkoré Region (q. v. ) which was to supply the sawmill at N'Zérêkoré built in 1964 by the Soviet Union.
Even with careful selective cutting and reforestation
this forest could not have supplied the plant's capacity
of 1. 75 million cubic feet a year and still have exported
lumber to the Soviet Union through Liberia as planned.
The few valuable species in the forest have been de-
cimated in the intervening years and the sawmill, if
operating at all, must be operating far below capacity.

**DIEPPE MERCHANTS.** The first French traders to trade
openly on the Guinea Coast despite Portuguese claims
to a monopoly of trade in all of Western Africa. By
1570 they had made contact with some coastal peoples
in what is today the Republic of Guinea.

**DINGUIRAYE.** A historical town and administrative region
of Upper Guinea located at the headwaters of the Tinkisso River (q. v. ) north of Dabola. The original retreat of the Fulbé leader Al Hajj Omar (q. v. ) in the
mid 19th century, Dinguiraye is a potential rich agricultural and cattle producing region.

**DUBREKA.** A town and region of Lower Guinea located just
inland from Conakry on the road north toward Boké.
Once an Atlantic trading center for products of the interior and later a banana producing center, Dubréka
now produces rice and palm nuts as well.

-E-

ECOLE GEORGES POIRET.  A vocational school for Africans
    opened by the French colonial administration in Conakry
    in the early 1930s.  It offered two- to four-year post-
    primary courses.  It trained only as many artisans and
    foremen as the French administration felt it needed.

ECOLE SUPERIEURE D'ADMINISTRATION (ESA).  An impor-
    tant part of the Institut Polytechnique Gamal Abdel Nas-
    ser de Conakry (IPC), this school of administration is
    charged with training political individuals for upper
    civil service levels.  The school was originally estab-
    lished in 1962 as the Collège Préparatoire d'Adminis-
    tration to train middle level officials, but was converted
    to a center for senior administrators under the name
    Ecole Nationale d'Administration in 1963.  In 1964 it
    became the ESA and in 1965 it was integrated into the
    IPC.

ECONOMIE MIXTE.  Economic goal under the Five Year
    Plan 1973-1978 in which "the people" assume control
    over formerly private capitalist enterprises.  Leader-
    ship was to be African, though some foreign private
    businesses would continue to participate.

ECONOMY  see  AGRICULTURAL PRODUCTION; ANIMAL
    HUSBANDRY; BANKING; CURRENCY; ELECTRICITY;
    FINANCES; FISHING; FOREIGN AID; FORESTRY; IN-
    DUSTRY; LABOR; MINING; PETROLEUM; PLANNING;
    TRADE--INTERNAL; TRADE--EXTERNAL; TRANSPOR-
    TATION

EDUCATION.  From 1968 on schools were renamed Centres
    d'Education Révolutionnaires (CER--q. v. ), which are
    work-study centers expected to contribute materially
    to national economic development.  Resembling similar
    centers in the People's Republic of China and in Cuba,
    the CER, especially in rural areas, are supposed to
    help create the cadres for socialist cooperatives.
        With the exception of Muslim Koranic schools, all
    education is nationalized.  Education from primary
    school to the university has been made available to more
    and more students since independence, although the
    goal of universal compulsory education has not yet been
    accomplished.  Most schools through secondary level,
    though, now have Guinean rather than foreign teaching

staffs and some success in Africanization of the curric-
ulum has been accomplished.

School organization consists of six years of primary school (first cycle), three years of lower secondary school (second cycle), three years of higher secondary school (third cycle); vocational and technical
schools are also on this level as is a new 13th grade
established in the 1973-1974 school year.  Course
length varies somewhat for the vocational and technical
schools.  Finally there are four or more years of the
fourth cycle, higher education (q. v. ).

As late as 1974 few urban schools operated on the
CER principles.  But 85 active CERs existed in 1972
at the level of the third cycle and 8,000 trained cadres,
mostly from rural areas, would have been ready to man
cooperatives in the fall of 1973 if the planned agricultural cooperatives had been ready.

ELECTRICITY.  Guinea has tremendous potential for hydroelectric development.  Currently only a small part of
this potential is harnessed.  Pita, Labê, Dalaba and
Mamou are served by the dam and power station built
by the People's Republic of China in the mid sixties at
the Kinkon gorge near Pita.  Conakry is also served
by a power station at the Grandes Chutes near Kindia,
which generates about 20,000 kilowatts.  Plans for a
hydroelectric station on the Koukoutamba, which enters
the Tinkisso, south of Kinguiraye are to furnish power
for processing the bauxite of Tougué and Dabola as
well as lighting the town of Dinguiraye, Siguiri, Labê,
Kouroussa and Faranah.  The Bokê bauxite project project promises increased use of hydroelectric power
produced on the Konkowi.  Thermal plants at Kankan,
Siguiri, Gaoual, Bokê, Sangredi and Kamsaru produce
114,000 or more kilowatts while small diesel genera-
tors operate part-time in many smaller towns.

ETHNIC CONFLICT.  Since many of the earliest political
groups in Guinea were ethnically or regionally based
there was intense ethnic rivalry until a Guinea branch
of the RDA (q. v. ) was founded in 1947.  Susu, Dia-
lonkê, Coniagui, Bassari and Badyarankê could remem-
ber that the Fulbê rulers had oppressed their ancestors.
Other ethnic groups also recalled historic animosities
and perhaps some lingering anti-Fulbê feelings still
plague the government but to a considerable extent the
PDG (q. v. ) and Sêkou Tourê have successfully overcome

ethnic differences and created a strong sense of Guinean nationalism.   See ETHNIC GROUP.

ETHNIC GROUP.   The term is best used to mean a group
   of human beings who, for the most part, have a common
   culture.   Unfortunately, European anthropologists and
   administrators, in order to distinguish among the various peoples of Guinea, conjured up muddled biological,
   historical and territorial groups which hardly corresponded
   to African perceptions.   Linguistic, cultural and historical groups do exist in Guinea but they are and have
   been constantly fluid.   Guinean nationalism is gradually
   superseding ethnic difference for many young people
   though a few major historical and linguistic groups
   still maintain considerable allegiance.   See ETHNIC
   CONFLICTS.

ETUDES GUINEENNES.   In 1945 the Institut Français d'Afrique Noire (IFAN--q. v. ), which had been created in
   1938 in Dakar, Senegal, established a Guinean territorial branch.   As director of this branch Georges Balandier founded and edited the branch's journal, Etudes
   Guinéennes.   This journal published original research in
   physical science, ethnology, economics and African culture and crafts from 1947 to 1956.   In 1959 the newly
   formed Guinean Institut National de Recherches et de
   Documentation (INRD--q. v. ) began publishing Recherches
   Africaines (q. v. ) as successor to Etudes Guinéennes.

EVOLUE.   An African who had sufficiently acquired French
   culture, in the eyes of the French, to be allowed to
   apply for citizenship.   In effect this meant giving up
   their own African culture for the few Africans who were
   ever granted this status.   Most Africans continued to be
   regarded as subjects rather than citizens throughout the
   colonial period.   See ASSIMILE; ASSIMILATION POLICY;
   INDIGENAT.


-F-


FAIDHERBE, GEN. LOUIS L. C.   French Governor of Senegal from 1854-1861 and from 1863-1865.   He was one
   of the designers of the early French foreign policy in
   West Africa.   He stopped Al Hajj Umar's expansion into
   the coast and laid the groundwork for the eventual French
   expansion into West Africa.

FARANAH.  A town and region of Upper Guinea located be-
     tween Dabola and Kissidougou on the border of Sierra
     Leone.  The birthplace of President Touré, this small
     and rather sleepy town has largely been by-passed by
     post-independence changes in the rest of the country.

FEDERATION DES ETUDIANTS DE L'AFRIQUE NOIRE EN
     FRANCE (FEANF).  An organization of politically aware
     African students in France who opposed the Loi-Cadre
     (q. v. ).  They offered support to Sékou Touré when he
     challenged the territorialist thrust of this law within
     the RDA from 1956 through 1958.  They, like Touré,
     wanted a West African federation of former French
     colonies rather than separate territories tied to France.

FILARIASIS.  A name given to a number of infectious di-
     seases caused by a string-like worm that lives as a
     parasite in human soft tissues.  River blindness (on-
     chocerca infection) is the most serious.  It is spread
     by the bite of a small black fly whose maggots are
     hatched in the fast flowing streams of Upper Guinea.
     Repeated infections over several years result in worm
     infections around the eyes resulting in blindness.  Be-
     cause the fly disperses so widely only massive cooper-
     ation with neighboring countries will allow Guinea to
     irradicate this disease.

FINANCES.  Critical to Guinea, as it is to any developing
     country, is the capital for financing development.  De-
     ficit financing of development projects through foreign
     loans, grants and trade arrangements has caused a
     tremendous inflationary pressure on Guinea's noncon-
     vertible currency.  Guinea has mortgaged its mining
     and export agricultural production for many years into
     the future and now can only hope that mining enter-
     prises like the Boké project can help the government
     of Guinea maintain solvency.

FISHING.  Guinea has an abundance of fish in both the
     rivers and along the coast.  These have long been used
     as an important food source.  Inland fishing is done
     with baskets, traps, poisons, hook and lines, and dyna-
     miting, though the last is supposedly outlawed.  Some
     4 to 5 thousand "barks" holding up to six fishermen
     and over 3,000 dugout canoes allow some 10,000 tra-
     ditional fishermen to earn a living in coastal waters.
     The larger barks are motor or sail equipped.  Three

mixed fishing enterprises with trawlers and refrigerator
boats also operate out of Conakry, producing over 9,000
tons of fish per year. These industries are owned jointly by the Guinean government and companies from the
United States, Japan and Kuwait. See SOCIETE NIPPO-
GUINEENE DE PÊCHE; SOCIETE GUINEE-KOWEITIENNE
DE PÊCHE.

FONDS D'INVESTISSEMENT POUR LE DEVELOPPEMENT
    ECONOMIQUE ET SOCIAL (FIDES). A law passed by
    the French Parliament on April 30, 1946, authorized
    creation of the fund to finance systematically and accord-
    ing to an overall development plan all of France's over-
    seas dependencies. The fund was to receive annual sub-
    sidies from the metropolitan budget and contributions
    from the territories concerned. After the independence
    vote of September 1958 Guinea no longer received any
    of this aid.

FONIO (Digitania exilis). Often termed a millet, this African
    cereal grain is the least productive of the grains raised
    in Guinea, but given dietary preferences developed since
    birth it is considered a special treat by many Guineans.
    Often giving little more than a two-to-one return for
    seeds planted and rarely as much as six-to-one, this
    nutrionally almost worthless cereal has little commer-
    cial value in world markets. It will grow in the poor-
    est of ground and is often planted on marginal land as
    an insurance against failure of the major grain crops
    like maize and rice. See MILLET.

FORECARIAH. A town and region of the same name on the
    Atlantic coast between Conakry and the Sierra Leone
    border. This region was formerly a major banana
    growing area with a small international shipping facil-
    ity at Benty. Largely overshadowed by Conakry in re-
    cent years it still has future potential as an important
    rice and palm production area. Its location on the
    Conakry to Freetown, Sierra Leone, axis should also
    prove economically advantageous.

FOREIGN AID. Published information on foreign aid to
    Guinea is uncoordinated and fragmentary but it seems
    clear that Guinea has received over $1.2 billion in
    foreign aid including private investment. Interest rates
    have ranged from loans from the Soviet Union and East-
    ern Europe at around 2.5 percent to direct credits from

the import-export bank at 7 to 8.5 percent. Guinea's
official and private foreign debt in 1971 was equivalent
to 84 percent of the country's 1970 GNP--one of the
highest rates of indebtedness in the world. Some
sources contend that Guinea's great mineral productivity is mortgaged for the next thirty years for debt
repayment. Having relied upon Western and Eastern
European, American, Chinese, Soviet and Israeli aid
since independence, Guinea has recently turned to a
number of Arab states for help. As one of the world's
25 least developed countries Guinea also should receive
some help from the United Nations Development Program in the future. Unless funds are better managed
and overall development plans better coordinated it is
unlikely that great strides in agricultural or industrial
output will soon be achieved under the present government.

FOREIGN RELATIONS. As a non-capitalist nation, Guinea
has found it ideologically easier to cooperate with Eastern European countries and the People's Republic of
China than with Western European countries, the United
States and Canada, yet pursue a stated policy of "pos-
itive neutrality." Guinea has found it theoretically and
pragmatically impossible to avoid accepting considerable
economic aid from Western bloc countries. In practice Guinea maintains a very closed and guarded stance
toward most nations. From their abrupt break with
France to the continuing periodic moments of patriotic
fervor generated by real and imaginary "plots" and
"aggressions," the psychological sense of being a nation
besieged by external enemies, both African and non-
African, is an important element of Guinean foreign
policy. National solidarity has, to some extent, been
achieved in Guinea by a paranoid "hot and cold" rela-
tionship with the rest of the world. See PLOTS.

FOREST REGION. One of the four geographic regions into
which Guinea is usually subdivided. The Forest Region
makes up the southeastern extension of Guinea. Its
major feature is the Guinea Highlands which range
from 1,500 feet above sea level in the west to over
3,000 feet in the east with some peaks of 4,000 feet
and more. Possessing some dense rain forest below
2,000 feet, much of the Forest Region is now derived
savanna and even the forest is largely secondary growth
because of the long presence of farming peoples in the
area.

FORESTRY.  Guinea has some teak and ebony trees as well
     as a few rubber and quinine plantations.  However,
     with the exception of locally used sawmill output, the
     lumber industry in Guinea has never been too produc-
     tive.  Less than 4 per cent of Guinea has substantial
     forest cover and valuable species have become very
     rare.  A sawmill at Nzerékoré and a particle board
     factory at Sérédou near Macenta have never operated to
     capacity and lumber reserves have been so depleted that
     it is unlikely they ever will.

FRENCH LANGUAGE.  French is the official language of
     Guinea along with eight national languages:  Poular,
     Maninkakan, Susu, Kissi, Guerzé (Kpelle), Toma, Con-
     iagui and Bassari.  Unfortunately, in spite of UNESCO
     help, literacy in national languages has been somewhat
     hampered by lack of funds for books and teachers.
     French thus continues to fill the need for administrative,
     technical and business communications inside the country
     and for inter-African and international relations.  It is
     understood by about 20 per cent of the population and is
     used as a lingua franca among educated Guineans of
     different ethnic groups.  It is the language of instruc-
     tion beginning with the fifth year of school and is taught
     from the third year.  It appears that French skills have
     declined in recent years since teaching personnel and
     students in Guinea suffer from an inadequate supply of
     books.

FRENCH UNION.  This structure was established under the
     French constitution of October 1946.  It allowed a mea-
     sure of representation for French colonial territories in
     the policymaking process of government.  The mainland
     African colonies were classified as overseas territories
     over which France felt it "must continue to exercise its
     domination. "  Only "evolved" (q. v. ) Africans were grant-
     ed full French citizenship.  Some African deputies were
     granted seats in the French National Assembly though,
     and elected territorial assemblies were given very lim-
     ited legislative powers in territory affairs.

FRIA.  A town and region of the same name located just in-
     land from the coast in lower Guinea between the Dub-
     réka and Boffa regions.  This town is a highly industria-
     lized "island" with its own railway line, oriented towards
     the outside world, with non-African technicians living
     totally independent from the African countryside.  Afri-

canization has been pushed by the government of
Guinea but the mining and aluminum processing industry is so important to Guinean finances that this enclave of European and American economic power continues to exist almost untouched by African direction.

FRONT POUR LA LIBERATION NATIONALE DE GUINEE
(FLNG).  A group of Guineans in exile opposed to
Sékou Touré's regime.  Like its counterpart the Association des Guinéens en France (AGF--q. v.) it is composed of university graduates, Guinean veterans of the
French military, former Guinean cabinet ministers and
a few former Guinean ambassadors.

FULBE (also Peul, Fulani or Foulah).  Claiming descent
from nomadic pastoralists in present-day Mauretania
the Poular speaking peoples are found largely in the
Futa Jalon in Guinea.  They are part of a large ethnic
group spread through much of West Africa from Senegal to Lake Chad in a belt between the rain forest and
the Sahara desert.  Members of this ethnic group created a relatively centralized state in the Futa in the
eighteenth century and maintained a dominant position
in the area almost until independence in 1958.

FUTA JALON ( Fouta Djallon).  A highland area in Guinea
with elevations up to 4500 feet.  It is the source of the
Gambia, Senegal and Niger rivers as well as a number
of other smaller rivers which flow directly south and
west into the Atlantic.  In the early 18th century, Fulbé
reformers created a theocracy there with the state controlled by elected almanies (q. v. ).  This Futa Jalon
experience served as a model for Islamic reformers in
other areas of West Africa.  The state of Futa Jalon
remained independent until the almany (q. v. ) placed it
under French protection in 1888.

-G-

GAMBIA RIVER.  This river gives the Gambia its name.
It rises northeast of Labé in the Futa Jalon and flows
northward toward the Senegal border and then on to
the Gambia.

GAOUAL.  A town and region of the same name in the Futa
Jalon highlands of Middle Guinea, between the Koundara

and Boké regions on the Guinea-Bissau border. This
region is seldom visited by visitors to Guinea because
of its inaccessibility and the fact that it served as a
staging area for anti-Portuguese guerrillas fighting to
free Guinea-Bissau. Potentially a rich agricultural and
cattle producing area, Gaoual remains largely undevel-
oped.

GARDE REPUBLICAINE.  A paramilitary organization of a-
bout 1,600 officers and men. Reinforcing the Gendarmerie, which policies the rural areas in administrative
regions, in Conakry the Garde provides the band and
the motorcycle escort for official welcoming ceremonies
as well as guarding the President's palace. One company guards Camp Alpha Yaya, the political prison near
the Conakry-Gbessia airport. See GENDARMERIE.

GENDARMERIE.  A paramilitary force of about 900 charged
with law enforcement, public safety and security throughout the country. At least one brigade of from six to
36 gendarmes commanded by a lieutenant or senior non-
commissioned officer appointed by the President is
assigned to each administrative unit. In the regions
along the country's border extra frontier brigades are
assigned to help the Customs Service. In Conakry
there are port, airport and city brigades as well as a
mobile detachment. Two criminal brigades, in Conakry
and the Futa Jalon, conduct investigations, take deposi-
tions, collect fines and make special reports in connec-
tion with specific infractions.

GOVERNMENT.  The Republic of Guinea is a single party
state in which executives, legislative and administrative power is tightly controlled by the President, his
prime minister and five other Ministers of Domain who
are also members of the the Bureau Politique National
(q. v.), the executive body of the Parti Démocratique de
Guinée (PDG--q. v.). Local and regional governments are
under the control of the minister of the interior and security. The 29 administrative regions have a governor
appointed by President Touré. Each region is divided
into arrondissements (q. v.) presided over by a commandant. At the local level, the Pouvoir Révolutionnaire
Local (PRL--q. v.), a party group whose chairman serves
as mayor, directs all governmental activities, including
production and consumption cooperatives, and is responsible to the commandant of the arrondissement and the

regional governor.    See PARTI-ETAT.

GRIOT.  A French version of the Wolof term gewel used for
persons whose responsibilities were to act as musicians,
historians, praise singers and advisors for Guinean rulers, especially among Mande speaking peoples.

GRIS-GRIS.  A slightly derogatory term applied to the leather
bound verses of the Koran which many Guinean Muslims
traditionally wore in much the same way Westerners
carry St. Christopher medals.

GUEKEDOU.  This town and region in the Forest Region
bordering on Sierra Leone and Liberia has long been
important in the production of coffee, rice, and palm
nuts.  Relatively densely populated, Guékédou is still
a rather isolated town in spite of its productivity.
Never of great importance in colonial times, Guékédou,
with little mineral wealth and connected with Macenta
and Kissidougou by very poor roads, had been drawn
very little into the national development programs.  A
tiny local soap factory closed in 1958 and reopened in
the 1960s represents Guékédou's sole non-agricultural
industry.

GUERZE (more properly called Kpelle).  An ethnic group
which in Guinea is mainly concentrated in the Nzérékoré
administrative district.  They are linguistically most
closely related to the Mende of Sierra Leone and thus
represent an ancient intrusion of more northern people
into the rainforest areas of the southwesternmost part
of western Africa.


-H-

HALCO.  A consortium formed in 1962 by Harvey Aluminum
Company to work bauxite deposits in the Boké region.
See BOKE PROJECT.

HARMATTAN.  A hot dry wind generated by the Saharan air
mass during the summer months.  It blows from the
interior to the coastal and forest regions of Guinea.
The effect of the harmattan is most intense in Upper
Guinea where it can cause the relative humidity to drop
from 70 per cent at night to 20 per cent by late afternoon.
Daytime temperatures also soar with the harmattan,

often exceeding 100° F. Vegetation dries as well as
peoples' skin, and dust fills the air on many days of
the harmattan season.

HEALTH. All institutions providing health facilities in Guinea
are run by the government. By 1970, there were 29
at least moderately equipped regional hospitals, com-
pared to the single one existing at independence.
Over 200 new dispensaries have been opened and the
number of doctors doubled. A school of medicine and
a school of pharmacy are supposedly now functioning.
It should be noted, though, that the ratio of doctors
to inhabitants remains about one to 37,000. Bad management, incompetent administration and drug and
equipment pilferage continue to hamper adequate health
care delivery. Equipment and supply shortages also
remain a severe problem. Preventive medicine can
hardly be said to exist. For most Guineans, hospitals
are a last resort and pharmacies and dispensaries
seldom can do more than apply dressings and dispense
a few drugs rather than actually provide adequate community wide health care and preventive medicine.

HIGHER EDUCATION. In 1961 Guinea nationalized all private educational institutions and required that post-
secondary scholars prove their "fidelity to the Party
and the country. " In 1962 the regime established a
polytechnic in Conakry. In 1968 the teacher training
institute L'Ecole Normal Julius Nyérêrê was upgraded
with the Conakry Polytechnic (then called L'Institut
Polytechnique Gamal Abdel Nasser de Conakry) to
form a national university with the following faculties:
social science, administration, electrical and mechan-
ical engineering, civil engineering, natural science,
pharmacy and medicine, agriculture, geology and mining. Textbooks and teachers are in short supply.
President Touré states that ideological formation of
teachers is more important than teaching excellence.
Consequently the quality of instruction and technical
competence of post secondary teachers leaves much
to be desired.
          Primary school teachers are trained in
Koba, Pita, Dabadou and Guékêdou and at more ad-
vanced schools in Faranah and Macenta. Besides the
secondary teachers graduating from the university,
the government sought in 1973 to construct two new
secondary teacher training institutes at Labé and Kin-

dia. Yet low pay, low morale and subsequent lack of
interest in teaching continued to plague teacher training programs throughout Guinea in the late 1970s.
See EDUCATION.

HOLY GHOST FATHERS. Founders of the first Catholic
mission in Guinea at Boffa in 1877. This Roman Cath-
lic order also established a number of schools in colonial times. Since the 1967 Africanization of clergy the
order has virtually ceased to function in Guinea. See
CATHOLIC MISSIONS.

HOROYA. Beginning in April 1961 this four- to eight-page
daily became Guinea's only newspaper. Officially an
organ of the PDG, it consists mostly of speeches and
statements by President Touré. Visits by foreign dig-
nitaries and information on economic and social developments are covered. Various government and Party
reports as well as full texts of important laws and de-
crees appear regularly. Guinean sports news also appears regularly. Occasionally international and African news items appear along with specifically signed
editorials and political poems. Circulation is somewhat more than 20,000.

HOSPITALS see HEALTH

HOUSING. Though in many areas European-style construction
with cement walls and floors and metal roofs has become the norm, many Guineans still live in one of
two types of traditional houses. In the forest a few
rectangular houses, their walls consisting of a lattice-
work woven frame coated with puddled mud, are still
constructed. Round houses of sun-dried brick supporting roofs of wood poles and thatch with a single wooden
door (and perhaps a single wooden shuttered window)
are the more common form of traditional housing.

HYDROELECTRIC POWER. Guinea has the greatest hydroelectric production potential of any nation in West Africa. Guinea has good rainfall and many fast flowing
streams which descend from the Futa Jalon (q. v.)
through deep and narrow valleys. Total potential is
estimated at 63.2 billion kilowatt-hours, of which one-
third is on the upper reaches of the Niger, 16 per cent
on the upper reaches of the Senegal River (Bafing) and
19 per cent on the Konkouré. Immediately harnessable

sources on the Konkouré, Tominé, Bafing and upper
Niger could yield 13.6 billion kilowatt-hours. Only
a small fraction of this potential is currently being
used but plans for harnessing more are numerous, as
adjuncts to ambitious plans for future production of
aluminum, iron and steel.

-I-

ILES DE LOS. A number of small islands five or six miles
southwest of Conakry in the Atlantic Ocean. They include Kassa with its now mined-out bauxite deposits,
Tamara with its excellent beaches, and Raume which
was once a slave trade and smuggling depot. This
latter island later became a British anti-slavery headquarters and perhaps inspired Robert Louis Stevenson's
description of "Treasure Island."

ILES TRISTÃO (Unhappy Islands). A number of small islands in the estuary of the Kogon River (q.v.) on the
border with Guinea-Bissau. These islands were named
by the Portuguese in the 16th century as were the Iles
de Los (q.v.) and other points along the Guinea coast.

IMPORTEX. A government agency formed in August 1975 to
take charge of the export-import trade. This is but
one of a long series of attempts to bring all trading
activities under governmental control.

INDIGENAT. A comprehensive set of violations and penal-
ties which were once basic to French colonial policy
in Guinea. Assuming under the policy of association
(q.v.) that most Africans could not measure up to the
standards of French culture required of African assim-
ilés (q.v.) who had adopted the French life style, the
French treated most Africans as subjects (see SUJETS
INDIGENES) rather than citizens. The French afforded strict treatment and fewer rights to the African
"subjects" under a separate legal regime. Established
by decree in 1924 the indigénat restricted African civil
liberties (e.g., rights of association and movement)
and permitted forced conscript labor or corvée (q.v.)
to build roads and other public works. French and
French trained administrators were given a free rein
to punish African subjects for violations as minor as
hindering traffic or responding disrespectfully to ad-

ministrators.  Condemned by administrators themselves at the 1944 Brazzaville Conference (q. v. ), the
indigénat was finally abolished in 1946.

INDUSTRY。  With the exception of the Fria mining complex
owned by a European and American consortium, Guinea
had little industry at independence.  A few privately
owned, small scale enterprises existed.  These concerns processed food (baking, canned fruit and juice,
beer, soft drinks, syrups and so on) or produced other light consumer goods like perfume essences, rain-
coats, sandals, metal construction materials, soap
and nails.  Many of these functioned at a seriously
curtailed level or ceased functioning altogether after
independence.

In the first fifteen years of independence a
number of industrial operations were created.  These
projects included a textile complex, two palm oil processing concerns, a canned fruit factory, a cigarette
and match factory, a canning plant, a slaughterhouse,
a military clothing and leather goods complex, a tea
processing plant, bicycle and truck assembly plants,
a tire recapping operation, and factories for the production of tiles, particle board and aluminum products.
A number of important mining firms have also been
created in the past 19 years.  All of these projects
are public or semi-public functions.

Many of the public and semi-public industrial
enterprises have been badly planned and very badly
managed.  Most were launched with insufficient pre-
paration。  Canning plants function far below capacity
because inadequate supplies of fruit, vegetables and
meat can be obtained.  Many Guinean managers are
ill-trained and incapable of running the enterprises to
which they are entrusted.  Furthermore industrial
"islands" like Fria have drawn workers from farming
and helped contribute to Guinea's total production defi-
cits.

Yet many projects still hold great promise,
especially those in the mining area.  Gradually better
trained and competent Guineans will perhaps lead to
better functioning of the state owned industries in the
future。

INSTITUT FRANÇAIS D'AFRIQUE NOIRE (IFAN).  Research
institute with headquarters in Dakar, Senegal, with
branches in most territories of French West Africa

founded in 1938. The Guinea branch was founded in
1945 by the French sociologist, Georges Balandier,
who also founded and edited the branch's journal, Etudes Guinéennes (q. v.), which appeared between 1947
and 1956. After independence the Institute's name was
changed to Institut National de Recherches et de Documentation (INRD--q. v.).

INSTITUT NATIONAL DE RECHERCHES ET DE DOCUMENTA-
TION (INRD). A Guinean national continuation of the
the Institut Français d'Afrique Noire (q. v.). Charged
with administering the national archives, national library, and national museums as well as a nature reserve at Mount Nimba, in 1959 INRD began publishing the quarterly journal Recherches Africaines as the
successor to Etudes Guinéennes (q. v.), previously published by the Institut Français d'Afrique Noire.

INSTITUT POLYTECHNIQUE GAMAL ABDEL NASSER DE
CONAKRY (IPC). In 1974 this institute of higher
learning in Conakry had 13 schools and faculties, including medicine and pharmacy. Along with the Ecole
Normale Julius Nyéréré in Kankan, it constituted the
national university, Established in 1962 with Russian
aid it concentrates on administration, science and tech-
nology for training personel to forward the industrial
and agricultural development of the nation.

INVESTISSEMENT HUMAIN. A kind of self-help program
launched by the Party in 1958. The "masses" were
mobilized to participate in development projects through
Party recruitment. By the end of the first Three Year
Plan (1960-1963), projects including hundreds of schools,
dispensaries, markets, mosques, roads and bridges
worth about 3 billion Guinean Francs had been completed through investissement humain. The coercion
necessary to continue this mobilization as well as numerous technical and administrative difficulties caused
the mass involvement program to be gradually abandoned in the 1960s. Many Guineans were disenchanted
when, after having worked on local schools and dispensaries, no teachers or nurses were made available
to staff them. Student and Army mobilization largely
replaced the investissement humain in the mid 1970's.

ISLAM. An Arabic word meaning "submission," it is the
name of the religion preached by the Prophet Muhammed

in the seventh century. A follower of Islam is a Muslim. Spread to West Africa by missionaries and traders in the ninth century, it flourished in the great West African Empires of Mali and Songhai as well as in the 18th and 19th century theocracies of Al Hajj Umar and Samory Touré. It is the dominant religion in Guinea today.


-J-


JEUNESSE DE LA REVOLUTION DEMOCRATIQUE AFRICAINE (JRDA). This youth organization of the Parti Démocratique de Guinée was declared as the single national youth institution in Guinea by the party leadership March 26, 1959. The JRDA concentrates on three areas of activity: culture and sports, national defence and "revolutionary" morale. As guardians of "revolutionary" morale, JRDA militants patrol hotels and dance halls against prostitution and "capitalist" music, manners and dress. Through the JRDA the PDG exercises control over all aspects of the performing arts and have forced a sterile conformity to a narrow definition of Guinean drama and music in order to remove "tainted" French and European standards. By giving officially approved focus to the recreational activities of young people and involving them in political work the JRDA has served as a training ground for future party leaders. Occasionally this "shock force of the revolution" has tended to outrun the adult PDG leadership and to present it with the task of keeping youthful impatience from changing into left-wing opposition. As Milices Populaires (q. v. ) JRDA members threaten to become an uncontrollable vigilante group persecuting any they defined as "enemies of the nation" according to their own whims.

JIHAD. A religious duty imposed on Muslims by the sharia or Muslim law for the maintenance of Islamic orthodoxy. Popularly known as "holy war" it is waged against apostates, threatening unbelievers, and enemies of Islam. See TOURE, SAMORY; MUSA, IBRAHIM; AL HAJJ UMAR.

JOURNAL OFFICIEL DE LA REPUBLIQUE DE GUINEE (JORG). The name under which the official journal of French colonial administration in Guinea was con-

tinued after independence. Appearing, more or less
regularly on a bi-weekly basis, it published laws, de-
crees, ministerial orders, notices of civil service
appointments and changes, and various other official
pronouncements.

-K-

KAMSAR. This small town on the Atlantic Ocean just south
    of Iles Tristão (q. v. ) on the Guinea-Bissau border be-
    came an important ore port and ore treatment center
    as part of the Boké project (q. v. ). In 1973 the com-
    pletion of an 85 mile railroad connecting the Sangrédi
    bauxite deposits with the coast at Kamsar made this
    small town into the second major port in Guinea over-
    night. Today, Kamsar is one of the most thriving in-
    dustrial towns in Guinea.

KANKAN. A town and region of the same name in Upper
    Guinea. The region borders on both the Ivory Coast
    and Mali. After Conakry, Kankan has the second
    largest population of any town in Guinea. A commer-
    cial, administrative and Muslim religious center of
    some importance, Kankan remains more a conglomer-
    ation of African villages than a modern Western style
    city.

KEITA, FODEBA. Born into a middleclass Maninka family
    at Siguiri in February 1921, he was educated at the
    William Ponty School. He studied law at the Sor-
    bonne but earned his living by writing poetry and short
    stories. As a radical, anti-colonial poet, his works
    were banned throughout French Africa from 1951 on-
    wards. He eventually abandoned the law to create the
    world famous Ballet Africain (q. v. ). Keita held cab-
    inet posts in the post-independence government of
    Guinea, but was sentenced to death for alleged com-
    plicity in the so-called "Labé Plot" (q. v. ). It is
    supposed he is now dead.

KEITA, NAMORY. Army chief of staff who replaced Nouman-
    dian Keita after the latter was purged for alleged trea-
    son in 1971.

KEITA, N'FAMARA. Born at Molota in the Kindia region in
    1924, he completed some secondary studies in Dakar

before becoming a court clerk in Macenta in 1947.
Picked by Touré as an active trade unionist, he rose
in politics as a member of the PDG and was elected
mayor of Kindia in 1956. Upon independence he was
appointed secretary of state in the office of the Presidency. In March 1960 he was appointed minister of
planning. Transferred to the Ministry of Trade in
January 1961, he served in that post, with other
brief assignments through 1972. He was minister of
the superministry of rural development in 1975.

KEITA, Gen. NOUMANDIAN. The chief of the combined
armed forces' General Staff, arrested in July 1971
after confessing to spying for the West German government in relation to the November 1970 invasion of
Guinea by Portuguese and a Guinean exile group, the
Régroupement des Guinéens en Europe (q. v.).

KEROUANE. This town and region on the headwaters of the
Milo River is the major diamond producing area of
Guinea. Between the savanna region of Kankan and
the forest regions of Macenta and Beyla on the border with the Ivory Coast, Kérouané remains a rather
isolated town. Historically this region on the flanks
of the Simandou Mountain range was the area from
which Samory Touré launched his short lived state at
the end of the 19th century. The region appears des-
tined to remain an economic backwater until hydroelectric resources, iron mining potential and better
transportation facilities are developed.

KINDIA. A town and region of the same name located between Dubréka and Mamou on the border with Sierra
Leone. The town was important in colonial times as
a trade and transportation center for plantation crops
and to a lesser extent still is so today.

KISSI. A relatively large rice growing ethnic group in the
Guékédou and Kissidougou regions. Other Kissi live
just inside the borders of Sierra Leone and Liberia.
Culturally and linguistically they are unrelated to the
dominant Mandé speaking populations to the north and
hence have been somewhat neglected in the political
and economic life of present day Guinea.

KISSIDOUGOU. Town and region of the same name in the
Forest Region south of Kouroussa and Kankan. Be-

tween the forest and savanna, the town of Kissidougou
has long been an important trade center. The region
is a rich agricultural area producing rice, coffee,
maize and other food crops.

KOGON RIVER. Rising in the Futa Jalon just west of Télimélé this river flows in a wide arch northwest and
then southwest to a large Atlantic estuary on the Guinea-Bissau border. Though it passes close to the major bauxite deposits at Sangarédi (q. v.) in the Boké
region, the river has yet to be named as a major
source of potential hydroelectric power.

KOKULO RIVER. One of three major tributaries of the Konkouré River, flowing from the Pita region toward Fria.
A dam and power station at the Kinkon gorge on this
river was completed by the People's Republic of China
in 1966; it supplies light to the towns of Pita, Labé,
Dalaba and Mamou.

KOLA NUTS (Cola nitida, or Cola acuminata). A golf ball
sized kernel traditionally traded by West African peoples. Containing considerable caffeine, this kernel
was a mild stimulant; commercially it is today used
in the production of cola drinks. The kola nut trade
in Guinea represented one of the principal trade items
in non-European trade especially between the Forest
Region and Upper Guinea.

KONO. A Mandé speaking people, a few of whom live in the
very southeast corner of Guinea. The majority of
this numerically small ethnic group live in the Ivory
Coast and Liberia.

KORA. A lute-harp or guitar which consists of half a large
calabash used as the soundbox and a long wooden pole
that protrudes from its rim to form the neck. It
usually has three or six metal or fiber strings, but
sometimes more. Such stringed instruments usually
were played by individual griots (q. v.).

KOUNDARA. A region and town of the same name in Middle
Guinea bordering on Guinea-Bissau and Senegal. A
rather isolated region producing peanuts, cattle, rice,
millet and maize, Koundara still promises to become
a major food-producing region in the future.

**KOURANKO.** A Maninka subgroup who live in the northern part of the Kissidougou region. These peaceful cultivators were probably originally a "caste" group within the larger Maninka ethnicity and today maintain a separate ethnic identity out of pride and self-respect.

**KOUROUSSA.** A town and region of the same name located in Upper Guinea between Kankan and Dabola. Located in what is largely a rice producing area of little importance in pre-colonial times, the town originally grew as an administrative center. It has become important as a transportation center with the arrival of the railroad in 1911 due to its position on the Niger River. When the railroad was pushed to Kankan, Kouroussa returned to its position as an administrative post with little other reason for existence.

**KPELLE.** The self-designation of the Forest Region ethnic group known in French as Guerzé (q. v. ).

-L-

**LABE.** A town and region of the same name in Middle Guinea between the regions of Mali and Pita with a northeast extension to the border of the Republic of Mali. Labé was an important commercial center in colonial times. The region produced coffee, oranges and jasmine essences (for perfume). With a relatively large population it has continued to maintain an urban air, though commercial activities have declined in recent years and have not yet been replaced by any large scale industrial operation.

**LABE PLOT.** In February 1969, President Touré, apparently fearful of an army coup like that which had overthrown the government of Modebo Keita in Mali, charged the army garrison at Labé with fomenting plans to seize national power. More than 1,000 Guineans were arrested in this so-called Labé Plot. Thirteen were executed and 27 were imprisoned, including high-ranking army and governmental officials. After this alleged coup attempt, the army's capabilities to act independently were severely curtailed and Party control was expanded. See PLOTS.

**LABOR.** Figures on Guinea's labor force vary greatly but

it would appear that less than 6 per cent of the ap-
proximately 2.6 million people between the ages of
15 and 64 are wage or salary earners.  Most of these
are probably employed by the government in administration (perhaps 22 per cent) and public enterprises
or other government sponsored activities.  The major
modern wage earning sector of the economy is the
Boké, Fria and Sangarédi bauxite mining enterprises.
Plantation employment has declined markedly since
independence and it is probable that subsistence agriculture production has grown rather than declined in
Guinea over the past twenty years.  Independent unions
are not allowed in Guinea and production brigades of
the type employed in the People's Republic of China
are often used to mobilize masses of the population
in public works projects.

LABOR UNIONS.  Independent labor unions, important before
     independence, no longer exist in Guinea.  The Con-
     fédération Nationale des Travailleurs de Guinée (CNTG)
     is now a government union.  It is headed by a cabinet
     minister with party militants holding all key posts at
     all levels.  At the top the CNTG links separate nation-
     al craft unions and professional organizations.  The
     same model is applied at the regional level.  In theo-
     ry local unions still exist but Party committees run
     even these.  See CONFEDERATION GENERALE DU
     TRAVAIL.

LANDOMA (also Landouma, Cocoli, Tyopi and Tiapi).  A
     people speaking a Baga dialect living inland from the
     Nalou between the Rio Núñez and the Fatala River to
     the west of Gaoual along the Guinea-Bissau border.
     Now largely integrated into the larger Susu speaking
     populations of the coast.  See BAGA.

LANGUAGE.  The official language of Guinea is French but
     after independence eight of the country's major ver-
     naculars were chosen as national languages.  These
     are Poular, Maninkakan, Susu, Kissi, Guerzé, Toma,
     Coniagui and Bassari.  Lack of funds has hampered
     attempts to teach people to read and write in these
     languages.  Only Susu, Maninkakan and Poular chall-
     enge French as languages useful in all of Guinea.

LEGAL SYSTEM.  For all practical purposes there is no
     autonomous legal "system" in Guinea at present.

What judicial authorities there are would seem to be
guided simply by the expedience of attempting to bring
about the interests of the PDG.  The chairperson of
the party unit at each level presides over courts at
that level.  At the arrondissement these courts handle
both civil and criminal cases.  Such is also the case
at the regional level, since there is an interlocking
membership on these courts.  A Superior Court in
Conakry serves as a final appeal in case of procedural
questions but this judicial body has no power to ad-
vise or judge constitutional questions.

Since the President has created quasi judicial bodies to convict persons accused of crimes a-
gainst the nation, the "system" exists only on paper.
The Supreme Revolutionary Tribunal which condemned
92 persons to death after the November 1, 1970, attack on Conakry allowed no defense testimony.  This
is perhaps more representative of the legal system
which now operates in Guinea than any description of
a theoretical scheme.

LOCAL ADMINISTRATION.  The local administration at the
village level is made up of the executive council of
the PDG whose president is also the mayor.  This
council is in charge, with political, administrative
and some judicial functions.  This local council is
empowered to employ party menbers to help keep
birth, marriage and death records, maintain roads,
dispensaries and sometimes cooperatives.  Above all
though, the local council's major duty is to mobilize
all citizens for projects elaborated by higher ranks
in the hierarchy.  See ADMINISTRATIVE ORGANIZA-
TION; ARRONDISSEMENT.

LOI-CADRE.  This enabling act passed by the French National Assembly on June 23, 1956, offered some
palliative reforms within the French colonial system.
It proclaimed universal suffrage and extension of a
single electoral college.  Of primary importance for
Guinea was a local executive council established in
Conakry with certain powers to run the administration
of the territory.  Control of this territorial assembly
became the immediate goal of the Guinean African
political parties, which turned from the more illu-
sive goal of participation in the politics of Metropol-
itan France.  Sékou Touré and his PDG gained control of this loi-cadre government.  This gave the

party the impetus to forge ahead and create a strong,
united Guinean party ready for self-government. The
law also helped assure the creation of separate, independent nation-states in former French West Africa
rather than the creation of a unified confederation.

LOS ISLANDS  see  ILES DE LOS

LOWER GUINEA.  One of the four major topographic areas
of Guinea, this coastal area is largely a plain, giving
way at its eastern borders to low hills, cut by deep
river valleys which in turn lead up to the higher es-
carpment of the Futa Jalon. Lower Guinea stretches
from 30 to 60 miles inland from the Atlantic Ocean.
Marshy islands and peninsulas help form a coast which
is deeply indented by brackish estuaries and dotted
with mangrove swamps forming the mouths of many
rivers. Heavy rainfall and warm tropical temperatures make this area an excellent rice and banana
producing area.

-M-

MACENTA.  A region in the Forest Region between Nzérê-
koré and Guékédou on the Liberian border. A forestry training center, particle board factory and a tea
plantation have been developed since independence.
The regional center is a pleasant town in rolling hills
supplied with adequate agricultural production.

MAIZE (corn; Zea mays).  A major subsistence crop throughout Guinea it is especially important as a food crop
in Middle and Upper Guinea. The regions of Mamou,
Siguiri, Koundara and Labé grow the largest amounts
but relatively little of this crop finds its way into the
market system. Rather self consumption and relatively low yields make this potentially important food
crop less important than it might be.

MALI.  A town and administrative region just north of Labé
on the Senegal border between the Koundara and Tougué
regions in the Futa Jalon. This region of 3,419
square miles has, as yet, contributed little toward national production. The region does have considerable
limestone which may perhaps be useful in the future
production of cement.

MALI EMPIRE. Two hundred years after the Berbers overthrew
the kingdom of Ghana, in the 11th century a Mandé-speaking ruler, Sundiata Keita, emerged from a village based
on the Niger in present day Guinea. Sundiata defeated other contenders for the military and commercial hegemony
of much of the west-central Sudan. On the base of
his conquests later rulers built the most powerful and
richest African empire in the area. The Empire last-
ed until the second half of the 15th century but the cultural influence and common sense of identity forged
by this empire continued on well into the 20th century.
See SUNDIATA; MANSA MUSA.

MAMOU. An administrative region and town of the same
name south of Dalaba on the Sierra Leone border between Dabola and Kindia. Long an important trade
center, its location on the crossroads of the east-west
axis between Conakry and Kankan and the route north
through Pita to Labé enhanced the importance of this
trading town in the colonial period. A center of fruit
and vegetable production, the region also boasts an
agriculture school and major meat and food processing industry.

MANINKA (Malinké, Manding). A Mandé speaking population
who claim to descend from groups who were once
united in the Mali Empire. Bearing clan names such
as Keita, Camara, Traoré, and Kourouma this ethnic
group is widespread in an arc of 800 miles from the
mouth of the Gambia River in the northwest to the interior of the Ivory Coast in the southeast. In Guinea
most live in Upper Guinea but as farmers, traders,
religious functionaries and bureaucrats they have come
to be a dominant ethnic group throughout Guinea.

MANINKAKAN. The language of the Maninka people.

MANIOC (Manikot utilissima). Also called tapioca and cas-
sava, manioc is a plant of American origin introduced
to Africa by the Portuguese. Its roots are eaten by
many Guineans when cereal grains are not available.
The young leaves of the plant are sometimes also used
as a vegetable. Though high in calories this starchy
food is poor in minerals, vitamins and protein. It is
filling, though, and constitutes an important part of
subsistence agriculture throughout much of the country.

MANO.   A relatively small ethnic group living to the east of
the Kpelle in the Nzérékoré administrative region.   The
majority of this Mandé speaking people live in Liberia.

MANSA.   A traditional Mandé title for the ruler of a mul-
tivillage polity.

MANSA MUSA (Ruled ca. 1307-1332).   Most famous of the
kings of ancient Mali largely because of his pilgrimage
to Mecca in 1324-1325.   On this pilgrimage his lavish
alms-giving of the great wealth in gold from the Buré
gold fields (q. v. ) made a lasting impression on the
Arabic chroniclers.   Mansa Musa represented a "gold-
en age" of ancient Mali, during which the literature of
the western Sudan grew and Sudanic architecture flourished.

MARABOUTS.   Muslim religious teachers who in some areas
of Upper Guinea came to exercise considerable political and economic influence.   In the households of African rulers who had accepted Islam there was usually
at least one marabout whose responsibilities in normal
times were to pray for the ruler, give advice, and
handle correspondence.   In colonial times, the term
came to apply to anyone claiming a modicum of Kor-
anic learning and/or Arabic literacy.

MIDDLE GUINEA.   One of the four reasonably clearly marked topographical regions of Guinea.   The region is
made up of a relatively high plateau called the Futa
Jalon (q. v. ).   Varying in altitude from 1, 500 to 4, 500
feet, most of the plateau is savanna covered with short
grass, interspersed with occasional clumps of brush,
baobabs (q. v. ) and even pines.   Rainfall is less here
than on the coast so the only heavily forested areas
are in the river valleys, which cut through the plateau in all directions.

MIFEGUI (Société des Mines de Fer de Guineé).   This proposed multi-national project for mining the rich iron
ore deposits of the Nimba-Simandou mountain ranges
includes Algeria, Nigeria, Zaïre, Japan, Spain and
Yugoslavia and possibly Rumania as partners with
Guinea.   This project also envisaged the construction
of a 675-mile trans-Guinean railroad from these mines
to a proposed deepwater ore port at Conakry for a
minimum cost of US $550 million.   See MINING.

MIGRATION.   Until the early 1960s farmers from Upper Guinea migrated to work on the peanut harvest in the Gambia and Senegal.   Some migration from Guinea to Sierra Leone and Liberia also took place, with young
men going to work for cash wages for a period and
then returning home.   Within the country Maninka
merchants regularly went from Upper Guinea to the
Forest Region to engage in small scale trading in rice
and other goods, while Fulbê cattle raisers moved
from valley pasturage in the dry season to plateau
pastures in the wet season.   A rather largescale shift
in population from rural areas to urban and mining
areas has also gone on since independence.   Finally
political disillusionment and economic pressure have
induced 600,000 to a million Guineans to leave their
country in search of better living conditions in Senegal
and the Ivory Coast.   A large number of such exiles
are also found in Sierra Leone, Liberia, Mali, the
Gambia and France.

MILICES POPULAIRES.   Beginning with Jeunesse de la Révolution Démocratique Africaine (q. v. ) volunteers who
sought out "opponents" of the party in the early 1960s,
this popular militia was made an organized civic service organization composed of young men and women
between the ages of 17 and 30 in the late 1960s.   By
1969 the militia was given small arms and military
training and given a role equivalent to the army.   In
1974 this militia was organized as a reserve force at
several levels throughout the country for national defense.   In Conakry it became a full-time regular force
and, throughout the nation Milices Populaires, organized in both combat units and as staff and cadre for
reserve militia units at the village and school levels,
were granted a status equal to the military and police.
In effect this second police  force was an attempt to
lessen the possibility of a military coup d'état.   But
by giving small arms to university and secondary
school students the government of Guinea may have,
inadvertently, created a potentially revolutionary force.

MILLET.   A number of drought-resistant cereal grains with
small round seeds enclosed in a hard outer coat which
occur in large numbers on short stalks at the top of
the stem.   Of little commercial value most of these
cereals are grown widely in Middle and Upper Guinea
on land too poor for maize.   They are a good source

of starch, but aside from some useful mineral salts,
contribute little more than bulk to the human diet.

MILO RIVER.  An important tributary of the Niger River in
Upper Guinea rising in the Simandou Mountains (q. v. )
just southwest of Beyla and emptying into the Niger
about 20 miles south of Siguiri.  Navigable by shallow-
draft barge from Kankan to the Niger, in colonial
times the river was a rather important avenue of
trade and commerce since it helped connect the rail-
heads of Kankan and Bamako.  With independence the
interregional flow of traffic has declined on the Milo.

MINING.  The most important mining operation is the Boké
bauxite project (q. v. ), which began in 1973.  This project operates under the authority of the Compagnie des
Bauxites de Guinée jointly owned by Guinea (49 percent) and a consortium of European and American companies.  Three other bauxite projects at Dabola, Kindia and Tougué are also planned.  The government of
Guinea also controls 49 percent of the Fria mining industry, which had operated as a private enterprise until 1973.  A multinational project called MIFERGUI
(q. v. ) for mining the rich iron ore of Nimba-Simandou
mountain ranges has also been planned.  Diamond-
bearing gravels as well as diamond-bearing pipes in
the area encompassed by Macenta, Kerouané and Beyla produced both industrial and gem stones.  No major gold mining or other major mining operation are
apparently now operating in the country.  See Table 2.

MOUNT NIMBA.  The highest mountain in Guinea, located
very near the border with Liberia and the Ivory Coast.
It is 5, 748 feet high.  See NIMBA MOUNTAINS.

MUSA, IBRAHIM.  A Muslim cleric who in 1725 launched a
Fulbé jihad (q. v. ) against other non-believers with the
help of some Dialonké (q. v. ) allies.  He died in 1751
but the jihad was continued by a military leader, Ibrahima Sori (q. v. ) and one of his descendants as almany (q. v. ).  The theocratic state envisaged by Ibrahim Musa has substantially influenced the history of
Guinea almost until the present.  See SORIYA; AL-
FAYA.

-N-

NAFOYA.   A state-run retail general store in Conakry.   See
    also SABOUYA.

NALOU.   A very small ethnic group which in colonial times
    lived on the lower Rio Núñez and on the Tristão Is-
    lands (q. v.).   They probably represent a remnant pop-
    ulation driven from the Futa Jalon by more organized
    Fulbé immigrants.

NENEKHALY-CAMARA, CONDETTO.   A poet and playwright
    who published a small volume of poems in France in
    1956.   His two plays, Continent Afrique and Amazou-
    lou, were published in France in 1970.   Amazoulou
    is an epic drama of the Zulu King Shaka and shows
    the strong bias toward historical African themes in
    government-approved artistic works in contemporary
    Guinea.

NEWSPAPERS  see  PRESS

NIANE, DJIBRIL TAMSIL.   A Guinean author and historical
    scholar of some note.   His Soundjata où l'Epopée Man-
    dingue, published in Paris in 1960 and translated into
    English in 1965 as Sundiata is an account of the found-
    er of the ancient Mali Empire based on oral traditions
    still extant in Guinea and modern Mali.   Niane collab-
    orated with Jean Suret-Canale in writing a history of
    West Africa in 1960.   He also contributed a number of
    articles to the scholarly journal Recherches Africaines
    in Conakry during the early 1960's.   A volume with
    two plays by Niane, Sikasso and Chaka, was published
    in France in 1971.

NIGER RIVER.   The fan-shaped drainage system of the head-
    waters of this great river, which originates in the
    Guinea highlands, drains over one-third of the country's
    total area including most of Upper Guinea and the Forest
    Region.   The fertile valley of this river has long been
    important agricultural producing areas of this part of
    West Africa but the massive flood control projects
    which would make these plains fully productive have
    scarcely been started.   Some few shallow-draft barges
    are used from Kouroussa to Bamako, Mali, on this
    river.

NIMBA MOUNTAINS. Located southeast of Nzérékoré on the
border with the Ivory Coast and Liberia, this mountain range is part of the larger Guinea highlands
stretching all across the Guinea forest zone. Major
deposits of magnetite (an iron ore) have been located
here and are being mined on the Liberian side of the
mountain range. In the center of this range is Guinea's highest mountain, Mount Nimba (q. v. ) at 5, 748
feet.

NZEREKORE. A region in the forest zone between Beyla and
Yomou on the border with both the Ivory Coast and
Liberia. Long isolated in the forest, the town of
Nzérékoré grew as an administrative, mission and
trading center after World War II. Today the region
boasts a sawmill and plywood plant as well as a growing population. The region has a relatively dense population and could produce a considerable agricultural
surplus. The future exploitation of the rich iron deposits of the region may someday make Nzérékoré a
major industrial area.

-O-

OFFICE DE COMMERCIALISATION AGRICOLE (OCA). An
institution created in 1970 to handle the selling of rural agricultural produce properly. The OCA buys agricultural produce from the farmers through the Pouvoir Révolutionnaire Local (q. v. ) at fixed prices set
by the government. Then the OCA sells these goods
to Importex (q. v. ), the government agency charged
with all import and export trade.

OFFICE NATIONAL DES CHEMINS DE FER DE GUINEE
(ONCFG). A national railway corporation which took
over the nation's only railroad at independence. This
road from Conakry to Kankan was in poor repair and
had been scheduled to be closed by the colonial administration. By 1967 only 140 of the 662 kilometers
from Conakry to Kankan had been repaired. Service
was cut to one passenger run a week from Conakry
and freight greatly reduced except for a few trains at
harvestime for the bananas of Coyah, Kindia and Mamou. A commuter shuttle continued to operate between Conakry and the suburb of Dixinn. Without
substantial changes in maintenance and management

the ONCFG will continue to operate at a greater deficit each year.

ORGANIZATION OF AFRICAN UNITY (OAU). In this pan-African body, founded in Addis Ababa in May 1963, Guinea has always been an interested member. Under the secretary-generalship of Guinean Diallo Telli from July 1964 to June 1972, it has led the African fight against colonialism and apartheid. It also sought to improve living conditions for refugees in Africa and settled some border conflicts. Under Telli the OAU failed most noticeably, though, in resolving the Nigerian-Biafran conflict.

OUASSOULOUNKE (Wasulunka). A self-identified ethnic group living east of Kankan in the southeastern part of Upper Guinea on both sides of the Mali border. They apparently were Fulbê (q.v.), originally conquered by Samory Touré (q.v.), who carved out a small principality for themselves in the last decade of the 19th century. See also MANINKA.

OUROUKORO. A small village between Kissidougou and Kérouané in the Forest Region where diamonds are mined in considerable numbers.

OUSMANE, BALDET. A former minister of financial control arrested and probably executed in 1971 following the invasion by Portuguese and Guineans in exile.

-P-

PALM OIL. One of Guinea's principal sources of cooking oils. Growing wild along the coast, oil palms are spared and helped to multiply. Serious plantation cultivation is not very widespread and most palm nuts are simply gathered from scattered trees when the price warrants the hazardous task of climbing the trees. Most oil is locally consumed while a relatively small number of palm kernels are exported.

PARK, MUNGO (1773-1805). Scottish explorer, sponsored by the African Association in 1795-1798 to investigate rumors concerning the Niger River. He traveled to the Niger near Ségou in present-day Mali and obtained some knowledge of the Mandé-speaking populations in

Upper Guinea. He probably drowned on a second expedition to the Niger in 1805 but he represented a
tangible beginning of the European drive to open up
the interior of West Africa.

PARTI DEMOCRATIQUE DE GUINEE (PDG). Founded as a
branch of the Rassemblement Démocratique Africain in
June 1947, this party has become the single legal party in Guinea. Beyond that it has, in effect, become
the government of Guinea. During the first few years
of independence the ideal of the PDG as the party of
the entire Guinean people was fairly accurate. What
actually exists today is an oligarchy of party elite
which struggles for power within the confines of an
increasingly autocratic control by the Life President,
Sékou Touré. See PARTI-ETAT.

PARTI-ETAT. Term used when referring to the nation or
the government. As President Touré explained it,
at first the People commanded the Party, and the Party controlled the State. Now the Party has become
identical to the State, or is the State.

PARTI PROGRESSISTE DE GUINEE (PPG). This party was
an outgrowth of the Group d'Etudes Communistes,
founded by a small group of French-educated intellec-
tuals. It was created in 1946 and dissolved in 1947.

PARTIDO AFRICÃO DA INDEPENDENCIA DA GUINE E DO
CABO-VERDE (PAIGC). The party founded by Amilcar Cabral (q. v.) which, in 1975, achieved the independence from Portugal of Guinea-Bissau. This party received support from the government of Guinea
throughout the 1960s and early 1970s.

PATESSON-ZOCHONIS (PZ). A British-owned firm which,
along with three or four other foreign firms, dominated commercial life in Guinea during colonial time.
These firms controlled the import-export trade, wholesale trade and some aspects of the retail trade until
state-controlled enterprise severely curtailed their
operations after independence.

PEANUTS (groundnuts). A spreading, fuzzy-stem annual le-
gume (Archis hypogosa) grown in many areas of Guinea. The plant was brought to Europe in the 16th
century from Brazil and later introduced to Guinea by

Europeans seeking a cash crop to exploit. Peanuts
are grown in all the natural regions of Guinea in
large fields as well as in subsistence plots. A small
surplus is marketed but peanuts do not represent an
important source of cash income in Guinea as they do
elsewhere in West Africa.

PETROLEUM. One of Guinea's major import needs is for
petroleum products as the nation has no known deposits of petroleum or natural gas. Guinea does, how-
ever, have a broad continental shelf, part of which
extends over 100 miles out to sea, and there remains
some possibility that oil deposits many yet be found
there.

PEUL  see  FULBE

PINEAPPLE (Ananas comosus). A plant of Central American origin which grows a juicy mass of 100 to 200
separate fruits at the apex of a cluster of long, thin
leaves with sharp edges. Planted from shoots it represents a potentially very important export crop for
Guinea. Most pineapples for export are grown on the
coastal plains since plantations in the interior face
severe transportation problems.

PITA. A town and region located north of Kindia and south
of Labé, between Dalaba and Télimélé. This heavily-
populated region possesses a major hydroelectric-pro-
ducing facility at Kinkon gorge on the Kokulo River
just below the town of Pita.

PLAN COMPTABLE NATIONAL. Plan to enforce socialism
in each sector of the economy by requiring strict ac-
countability. Covers industry, commerce, agriculture
and cattle-raising, banking, transportation.

PLAN QUINQUENNIAL (1973-1978). The latest of three economic plans. This five year plan follows the Three-
Year Plan, 1960-1962 and the Seven Year Plan, 1964-
1970. The five year plan focuses on the production
of material goods needed for national well-being, especially agricultural development and the formation of
state-private enterprises. Party activists played a
large role in producing the plan--a plan which calls
for a large degree of mass participation in the form
of work brigades. The plan called for the formation

of 200 such work brigades in 1974, 3,000 in 1975
4,500 in 1976, 5,500 in 1977 and 7,125 in 1978.   See
BRIGADES DE PRODUCTION.

PLANNING.   Guinea has attempted since 1960 to operate under a centrally-planned economy.   The first plan, the
Three Year Plan, 1960-1962, was prepared by a team
of French experts.   Its major decision was to create
an independent Guinean currency.   Lacking adequate
administrative machinery, this first plan had little
effect.   The second plan, the Seven Year Plan, 1964-
1970, was based on lists of needs compiled throughout the country by party institutions.   Economic analysis was lacking and most of the projects listed proved
unfeasible.   The third plan, the five-year Plan Quin-
quennal, 1973-1978 (q.v.), attempted to involve both
party institutions and adequate technical advice.   Formally launched on October 2, 1973, this plan would
seem more likely to achieve some success than its
two predecessors.

PLOTS.   A special dimension of Guinea nationalism is what
Guinean leaders refer to as the "permanent plot."   According to this view, since independence in 1958 there
has been a permanent plot against the PDG-led government of Guinea.   From the first alleged plot in April
1960, which was to be led by French troops, to the
apparent Portuguese involvement in an invasion in November 1970, the Guinean regime has expressed fear
of "imperialist" and "neo-colonial" schemes to overthrow the government.   Some of these fears may simply be an attempt to mobilize mass support but some
fears might be well-founded.   More than 600,000 Guinean exiles and other anti-Touré forces do exist in
neighboring countries and elsewhere.

POLITICAL PARTIES.   After Independence only one party
remained, the Parti Démocratique de Guinée (PDG--
q.v.).   Replacing a number of overseas affiliates of the
major parties in France and parochial parties of ethnic or regional nature which had existed from the end
of World War II, the PDG found its base in labor unions, youth groups, women's organizations and even
veterans groups but represented the whole territory of
Guinea including the great "peasant" mass.   The outspoken call for colonial reform which the PDG made
throughout the 1950s gave it great support which the

other more moderate and elitist parties could not mus-
ter.  This, coupled with a far greater skill at mobil-
izing all segments of the Guinean society and finally
the decision to vote for independence from France on
September 28, 1958, left it the only viable party on
Independence Day, October 2, 1958.

PORTS.   Only two international ports of entry exist in Guinea.
The facilities at Conakry, though poorly maintained and
managed are probably sufficient for the nation's present
needs.   The harbor itself is one of the best in West
Africa but is badly subject to silting.   One ore-load-
ing dock, maintained by foreign technicians, functions
quite well.   A second subsidiary port has been developed at Kamsar (q.v.) in recent years to handle the
export and import requirements of the Boké project
(q.v.), a bauxite industrial unit.   Smaller coastal
ports which once carried on some trade are now of
little importance.

POPULATION.   An official government census in 1972 fixed
Guinea's population at 5,143,284.   United Nations figures and foreign governmental organizations placed
the total between 4.1 million and 4.2 million in 1972.
The larger figure would seem to include Guinean-born
persons who were not actually residing in the country
as of December 31, 1972.

POULAR.   The language of the Fulbé (Fulani) people.

POUVOIR REVOLUTIONNAIRE LOCAL (PRL).   Refers to the
local organization of party and government officials
who direct economic, political, social, and cultural
affairs at the village level.   President Touré calls
the PRL real socialism, because the power of decision over all services and goods is theoretically
in the hands of the people at the local village level.

PRESS.   Printed media in Guinea under the colonial regime
was limited.   At independence only a half dozen newspapers and periodicals were published.   At present
only the party daily, Horoya (q.v.), the party weekly,
Horoya-Hebdo and the government Journal Officiel de
la République de Guinée appear on anything approach-
ing a regular basis.   The Agence Guinéenne de Presse
(AGP), Tass and Novosti Press Agency are the press
bureaus in operation at this time.

PROTESTANT MISSIONS.  Protestant missionary activities in
    Guinea were rather limited even in colonial times.
    Today no more than 1,000 converts of a few American
    missionaries and a few Anglicans. make up the entire
    Protestant community.  The Church Mission Alliance
    operations in Guinea, which once included a boarding
    school for children of missionaries near Mamou and
    a vocational education center near Kissidougou, seem
    to have been terminated in the late 1960s.


-Q-


QADIRIYYA.  The chief Muslim tariq (literally, way) or
    brotherhood in Western Africa in the 19th century.   It
    was the first such tariq formed to make the doctrines
    of Islam more intelligible to the ordinary believer,
    and was created by Abd al Qadir al Gilani in the 12th
    century.  Today in Guinea only the Diakhanké at or
    near Touba belong to this brotherhood.

QUININE.  A drug obtained from the bark of the cinchona
    tree.  Once a relatively important substance for the
    suppression of malarial attacks, the production of
    quinine in the Forest Region of Guinea is now prac-
    tically abandoned.

QUINZAINE ARTISTIQUE.  An annual arts festival lasting
    two weeks, which, since its founding in 1964, the Par-
    ty has used in an attempt to develop a unified nation
    cultural heritage as part of national development.
    Theatre, traditional music, modern music, painting
    and decorative design and folklore supported by Party
    institutions from all over Guinea are judged on the
    basis of their contribution to party ideology and artis-
    tic excellence.  Since 1969 the festival had attracted
    increasing numbers of foreign delegations.  In 1973
    the competitions were observed by delegates from Li-
    beria, Gambia, Zaïre and many Eastern-bloc countries.


-R-


RAILROADS.  The railway line linking Conakry with Kankan
    is badly in need of upgrading beyond Kindia.  (See
    OFFICE NATIONAL DES CHEMINS DE FER DE GUINEE).
    The line to the bauxite works in Fria is in reasonable

repair. The 135-kilometer line which links the Boké
bauxite deposits with the new deep-water port at Kamsar has an excellent heavy-gauge roadbed and should
prove quite durable. The projected 1200-kilometer
Conakry-Mount Nimba railroad for iron ore export
seems unlikely to be built in the near future.

RASSEMBLEMENT DEMOCRATIQUE AFRICAIN (RDA). An
African inter-territorial movement founded at Bamako
(in present-day Mali), in 1946. Its manifesto demanded
the constitutional confirmation of the rights of all people in the French overseas possessions. It also called for the peaceful, parliamentary elimination of colonialism throughout the world.
    Originally, part of the RDA, the Parti Dém-
ocratique de Guinée (q. v.) severed its ties with its
parent organization on October 19, 1958. Guinea's
rejection of the Constitution of the Fifth French Republic went against the idea of a closer union with
France which other RDA members supported.

RAY, AUTRA (Mamdou Traoré). A poet and intellectual supporter of the Touré regime who fell out of favor with
the government in November 1961 and no longer
appears to be a major voice in Guinean letters.

RECHERCHES AFRICAINES. A quarterly journal of the Institut National de Recherches et de Documentation
(q. v.). This is an "in-house" publication which of-
fers a means for the organization's small research
staff and the few other Guineans engaged in social
and natural science research in Guinea to publish
their works. It is a successor to Etudes Guinéennes
(q. v.).

REFUGEES. The increasingly repressive measures adopted
by the government of Guinea in the 1970s continued
to swell the ranks of those who had already left the
country for political and economic reasons in the 1960s.
There are more than 600,000 persons of Guinean origin living in exile at present. (Some sources suggest
figures as high as one million or more.) A great
majority of these people are living in the countries
immediately bordering Guinea. Most of these exiles
are to be found in the Ivory Coast and Senegal. But
substantial numbers, especially those with higher education and skills, can be found in France and else-

where outside of Africa. Two political groups have
existed among Guineans in exile--the Front pour la
Libération National de Guinée (FLNG) and the Association de Guinéens en France (AGF)--neither of
which have posed much real threat to the Touré regime.

REGIONAL ADMINISTRATION.  Guinea is divided into 29 administrative regions.  Each of these regions is under
the authority of a governor appointed by the president.
Each governor has three secretaries general: one for
economic affairs, one for social affairs and one for
fiscal control.  In theory each of these administrative
regions has a party-elected council which approves the
regional budget.  It would appear that this regional
level of government is where most central government
controls are exercised and most services dispensed.

RICE (Oryza sativa).  The most important cereal grain grown
in Guinea.  An annual plant of the grass family, it
is a good producer, especially in the paddy variety,
but Guinea continues to suffer from a chronic shortage of this important food crop.  With little use of
largescale irrigation and tractors the ricelands of
Lower, Middle and Upper Guinea have not achieved
their potential in the years following independence.

ROADS.  Like most West African countries, Guinea has a
rather incomplete road system.  There are more than
28,400 kilometers of roads and tracks in the country
but less than 12,400 of them are passable by regular
vehicular traffic.  Only about 520 kilometers of road
are hard surfaced and even these are not always in
good repair.  Motor vehicles are relatively few in
number and often in poor repair throughout Guinea,
because of import restrictions and poor maintanence
facilties.


-S-


SABOUYA.  A state run retail general store in Conakry.
See also NAFOYA.

SANGARE, TOUMANE.  A stalwart supporter of Touré, San-
garé has always managed to avoid being associated
with smuggling operations or coup attempts.  He was

the governor of the Guêkêdou region through much of
the 1960s and drove the important rice-producing
area to continued production in spite of transportation difficulties and a shortage of agricultural equipment and supplies. He was appointed to a ministerial position in the 1970s and continues to exert considerable influence upon the presidency.

SANGAREDI. The site of one of Guinea's five or six major
exploitable bauxite mines. Mining operations began
at this location on the Kogon River in the Boké region in August 1973. The government of Guinea hopes
to export 9 million tons of bauxite a year from this
location when full production is reached.

SATIYO-TIYO. Village head, a Maninka word which literally
means owner of the land. He was normally the eld-
est member of a lineage recognized as having titular
rights to this office.

SAVANNA. A tropical grassland region where rainfall is
seasonal and there is one long, dry season. A number of grasses form the main vegetation along with
trees and shrubs that vary in kind and number according to the climate and soil. The Guinea savanna
ranges from the rainforest along the coast and the
forest region to the northwest borders with Mali and
Senegal where only scattered baobab and acacia trees
break up the carpet of grass (Chechrus biflorous).

SECTION FRANÇAISE DE L'INTERNATIONALE OUVRIERE
(SFIO). This French socialist group gave considerable support to African politicians in the early 1940s.
This support was never as important in Guinea as it
was in neighboring Senegal. Fulbê students from Guinea at the Ecole Normale William Ponty were closely
associated with the SFIO but the French socialist influence never gained widespread support among the
majority of Guineans.

SENEGAL COMPANY. A short-lived, but important commercial company established by the French in 1672. In
1677, a French fleet captured Gorée, an island just
off Cape Verde in Senegal, from the Dutch. Using
this as the main base of operations, the company,
in conjunction with French naval vessels, harassed
the shipping of the British Royal African Company.

The company established some posts south toward Guinea but war in 1689 caused them to give up their monopoly, first to the Guinea Company and finally in 1696
to the Royal Senegal Company.

SHEA-BUTTER TREES (Butyrospermum parkii).  A semi-
cultivated tree which grows in the Upper Guinea savanna.  The Shea tree produces a large, white kernel
which is rich in oil, or shea butter.  When palm and
peanut (groundnut) oil are lacking or too expensive,
shea butter is used throughout Upper Guinea for cooking, making candles, ointments and soap.

"SHOPKEEPER'S PLOT" (Trader's Plot).  One of some dozen
or so alleged attempts to overthrow the government.
Plots such as this, whether real or imaginary, are
used as occasions for arousing the patriotism of the
Guinean masses in support of the regime.  In this
particular case merchant groups who were unhappy
with trade restrictions and nationalization of retail and
wholesale trade were accused in 1965 of seeking to replace President Touré's government with a French-or-
iented one.  Some external support from French commercial and governmental interests may possibly have
been involved.

SIGUIRI.  A town and administrative region in Upper Guinea
on the border with Mali.  Bordering on the regions of
Kankan, Kouroussa and Dinguiraye, this area was historically an important gold-producing center.  The
French colonial regime planned to make use of the extensive Upper Niger plains in the Siguiri region as a
major rice-producing area but since independence such
plans have languished.

SIMANDOU MOUNTAINS.  A range of mountains running north
and south between Beyla and Kérouané in the southeastern Guinea highlands.  These mountains contain major
deposits of magnetite, a rich iron ore which may eventually make Guinea a leading exporter of iron ore if
transportation and capital costs can be met.

SLAVE TRADE.  Domestic servitude was an indigenous institution among most people of Guinea.  It was con-
verted by the Atlantic slave trade into a much larger
and mutually profitable business for some Africans and
Europeans.  The Portuguese in their earliest voyages

captured slaves, but not until the plantation economies
of the Western Hemisphere developed in the 16th century did the slave trade achieve major importance.
The earliest English and French traders to Guinea
were not interested in slaves but in the 18th century
fairly large numbers of slaves were shipped from areas on the Guinea coast. British abolition in 1807
dealt a major blow to the Atlantic slave trade, though
some slave ships called in the area for the next twenty years. The British presence at Victoria and the
Iles de Los was part of the British anti-slavery movement in the early 19th century, which declined after
1850. Domestic servitude of various forms continued
in Guinea until well into the 20th century.

SMUGGLING. Guinean currency is non-convertible the regime sets fixed prices on agricultural goods and basic
necessities are often unavailable; therefore, smuggling
has constituted a continual problem since independence.
Agricultural products produced in Guinea are sold in
Mali, Senegal, Liberia, Sierra Leone and the Ivory
Coast for reasonably high prices in convertible currency. Consumer goods are in turn smuggled in to
be sold at high profits which in turn are used to buy
more agricultural goods. Guinea's long, permeable
borders have thwarted governmental attempts to stop
such clandestine traffic.

SOCIETE AFRICAINE DES PÊCHES MARITIMES (Afrimar).
A mixed enterprise fishing venture begun in 1973.
KLM, the Dutch airline, furnished the capital for this
venture and retained 51 percent ownership while taking
35 percent of the profits. The Guinean government
held 49 percent of ownership and took 65 percent
of the profits. This company was managed by a United
States fishing firm.

SOCIETE COMMERCIALE DE L'OUEST AFRICAIN (SCOA).
One of the most important of the foreign firms which
dominated commercial life in Guinea during colonial
rule. Firms like this one largely controlled the import-export trade and wholesale trade of the colonies.
This company was largely Swiss owned.

SOCIETE GUINEENE DE PETROLE (SOGUIP). A joint enterprise created in June 1974 with the American oil
company, Buttes Resources International, which was

to prospect for oil in a 17,000-square-mile area of the
Guinean offshore continental shelf. The Guinean government held 49 percent of the shares and the American firm held 51 percent while Guinea was to receive
63 percent of eventual oil profits.

SOCIETE GUINEO-KOWEITIENNE DE PÊCHE (Souguikop). A
mixed enterprise fishing venture started in 1973 with
two trawlers. The Guinean government received 49
percent ownership and 65 percent of the profits in
return for fishing rights in its coastal waters. The
government of Kuwait furnished the capital in return
for 51 percent ownership.

SOCIETE INDUSTRIELLE ET AUTOMOBILE DE GUINEE
(SIAG). One of the trading firms which literally con-
trolled Guinean commercial life during colonial times.
This particular, largely French-owned company prac-
tically monopolized automotive imports into French
Guinea.

SOCIETE NATIONALE D'ASSURANCE (SNA). One of the many
national financial institutions created after independence
to replace the French-controlled institutions which existed in colonial times. This national insurance enterprise became the sole insurance-granting institution in independent Guinea.

SOCIETE NIPPO-GUINEENE DE PÊCHE (Sonigue). Another
mixed enterprise fishing venture which operates pro-
specting boats, two fishing boats, and a refrigerator
ship. The Guinean government received 49 percent
ownership and 65 percent of the profits in return for
fishing rights in its coastal waters. Japanese capital
supplied the ships and technical management. See
also SOCIETE GUINEO-KOWEITIENNE DE PÊCHE.

SOCIETES INDIGENES DE PREVOYANCE (SIP). Pseudo-
cooperatives organized by the French government in
the 1930s as a means of improving agricultural productivity. The full title of these "cooperatives"--So-
ciétés Indigènes de Prévoyances de Secours et des
Prêts Mutuels Agricoles--more clearly reveals their
intent. They were governmental commodity credit
associations with little if any cooperative aspects.

SONINKE. The ethnic group which constitued the basic pop-

ulation of the ancient empire of Ghana. Many devout
Maninka-speaking Muslim scholarly lineages in Guinea
claim to be descended from Soninké ancestors.

SORI, IBRAHIM. The secular military leader who succeeded
Ibrahim Musa (q. v.) as leader of the Fulbé Islamic
state in the Futa Jalon about 1751. Sori managed to
firmly establish Fulbé control over the Futa and some
surrounding territories by the late 1770s. When Sori
died in 1784 the clerical supporters of the family of
Ibrahim Musa, the Alfaya (q. v.), and the military part,
the Soriya (q. v.), which supported Ibrahim Sori's descendants, kept the Futa divided in civil war until the
French occupation in 1897.

SORIYA. After the death of the successful jihad leader, Ibrahim Musa (q. v.), in the mid-18th century Futa Jalon, two rival factions developed. The military party
favored the descendants of the war leader Ibrahim Sori
(q. v.). This group was called the Soriya. The clerical supporters of the family of Ibrahim Musa were
called Alfaya (q. v.). These two groups contended for
the position of almany (q. v.) in the Futa Jalon until
well into the 20th century, though succession was in
theory fixed by the French after 1897.

SUDAN. The Bilad as-Sudan of Arab writers literally means
"land of the blacks." This term has generally been
applied to the vast area of the savanna stretching from
the Atlantic to the Red Sea between the Sahara desert
and the tropical rainforest to the south, but more especially that part west of Lake Chad where Islam and
largescale states were long known to writers in Arabia. Much of Upper Guinea is part of the Sudanic
world.

SUJETS INDIGENES. So-called "native subjects" in colonial
times. This status denied Africans the right to vote,
made them subject to disciplinary measures without
trial for "disrespect" or refusal to perform minimal
tasks for white administrators. All but a very few
Africans remained in this status through French colonial rule. See INDIGENAT; ASSIMILES; EVOLUES.

SUNDIATA KEITA. The son of a small Maninka authority
in Upper Guinea who defeated the Susu rulers of Kum-
bi-Saleh (ancient Ghana) in about 1235. By his death

in 1255 he had laid the foundations for the great Mali
Empire which he ruled from his capital, Niane, near
the present border of Guinea and Mali.  See MALI
EMPIRE; MANSA MUSA.

SUSU (also spelled Sosso or Sousou).  A Mandé-speaking
    people whose culture has gradually supplanted those
    of other ethnics in the coastal areas of Guinea in the
    past three hundred years.  Susu is now the lingua
    franca of most residents of Lower Guinea.  The Susu
    who are still predominantly cultivators and traders
    probably originated in the savanna of present-day Mali
    and Upper Guinea.  Susu are now one of the three
    major ethnic groups in Guinea.

SYLI.  The basic unit of Guinean currency since October 2,
    1972.  One Syli was equivalent to ten Guinean francs
    and was made up of 100 couris (cowries).  Officially
    rated at 20.46 sylis to the dollar, the clandestine rate
    of exchange approached 180 per dollar in the mid 1970s.

SYLIART.  A civil society created by the government of Gui-
    nea in July 1971 to subsidize and regulate the works
    of authors and producers in the Republic of Guinea.
    Granted a capital of 10 million Guinean francs this
    society was to operate on revenue derived from au-
    thorship rights, receipts from productions, artistic
    and cultural shows and state grants.  It was also to
    provide pensions for retired artists.  In May 1973
    Syliart was replaced by the Agence Guinéenne de Spec-
    tacles (q.v.), a public institution under the Ministry
    of Youth, Arts and Sports.


-T-


TALL, AL HAJJ UMAR.  The leader of the Tijaniyya tariq
    (q.v.) in the western Sudan, was born about 1790,
    educated in Senegal, and later traveled widely includ-
    ing a five-year pilgrimage to Mecca.  Coming under
    the influence of Ahmad al Tijani, whose teachings he
    accepted, he lived in the Muslim state of Sokoto in
    northern Nigeria until 1838 when he established a re-
    ligious and military base at Dinguiraye in Guinea.
    By 1852 he launched a jihad (q.v.) against the Bambara
    and by 1863 he controlled the territory from the up-
    per Senegal River to Timbuktu.  Only French colon-

ial opposition kept him from creating a powerful Muslim state in the headwaters of the Senegal and Niger Rivers.

TARIQ. Literally, the "way." A group of individuals who subscribe to a common Muslim philosophy and ritual. The two most celebrated tariqs in West Africa were the conservative Qadiriyya (q. v.) and the Tijaniyya (q. v.). The latter, founded in 1781, was a far more proselytizing group which called forth more active application of Muslim principles and hence helped mobilize large numbers of followers in Upper Guinea in the 19th century.

TCHIDIMBO, RAYMOND. The Roman Catholic archbishop of Conakry since 1961 when the French archbishop was expelled. Tchidimba's mother was Guinean, while his father was Gabonese. Tchidimbo was accused of involvement in the coup of November 22, 1970, against Sékou Touré and condemned to life in prison. See PLOTS.

TEACHER'S PLOT. An alleged plot against the government announced by Guinean leaders in November 1961. Basically teachers were complaining about working conditions but some of the documents presented by the pupils demonstrating in support of the teachers contained some leftwing ideological criticisms of the government. Among these statements were those suggesting that Guinea had to choose between Eastern-bloc and Western-bloc support. Touré ordered the expulsion of the Soviet ambassador suggesting that the ambassador was supporting teachers' demands that the Guinean government become a member of the Eastern bloc. The Soviet role in the strike has never been verified but five members of the teachers' union were executed and others fled or were imprisoned. See PLOTS.

TELECOMMUNICATIONS (see also VOIX DE LA REVOLUTION). In 1971 there were about 7000 telephones in the country but upkeep of lines was poor. Telegraphy linkages between regional capitals were also erratic since communications personnel often were forced to leave their work to search for food and other necessities due to the chaotic state of commercial distribution networks throughout the country. In February 1974, the African Development Bank granted Guinea a loan

equivalent of $4.8 million to upgrade telecommunica-
tions throughout the country according to a plan drafted with the help of the International Telecommunications Union.  The project included installation of mi-
crowave relays south toward Sierra Leone and throughout the country.  This plan also provided for the expansion of the automatic telephone exchanges of Conakry, Kankan, Kassa and Sonfonya.  Progress on the
projects has been very slow.

TELIMELE.  A region and town between Pita and Boké on
the western slopes of the Futa Jalon.  The town of
Télimêlê had been a small village in 1959 but by 1967
had grown to 12,000 as an administrative region capital.  With cattle raising as its major industry the region is of relatively little economic importance.

TELLI, BOUBACAR DIALLO.  Born at Porédaka in the Mamou region, he earned a doctorate in law in Paris in
1947.  He served as assistant public prosecutor in
Senegal and Dahomey.  In 1957 he became secretary-
general of the Grand Council of West Africa but when
Guinea voted for independence in 1958 Telli returned
to Guinea.
        He served as Guinea's permanent represen-
tative at the United Nations (1958-1964) and ambassador in Washington (1958-1961).  He was elected the
first secretary-general of the OAU on July 21, 1964,
and served in that capacity until June 1972.  Appointed minister of justice in August 22, 1972, Telli
was able to convince Touré that he was still a loyal
party member after his long absence from the country and remained one of the few Fulbé representa-
tives in the government until August 1976.  At that
time he was accused by President Touré of complicity in a plot against the government.  This fact, a-
long with his apparent ill health effectively removed
him from political power.

TIJANIYYA.  A Muslim tariq or voluntary brotherhood,
founded in the late 18th century in North Africa.  A
far more popular and active form of Islam it generated large followings in the 19th century and formed
the ideological basis of Al Hajj Umar's theocratic
state in the 1850s.

TIMBER.  Less than 4 percent of Guinea is covered with

valuable woodlands and species like teak and ebony
have almost totally disappeared. Without massive re-
planting and careful management it is unlikely that
Guinea will ever produce very much timber.

TINKISSO RIVER. Rising in the Futa Jalon between Dabola
and Mamou this river is one of Guinea's main tributaries of the Niger River. It flows into the Niger
at Siguiri. It is a potential source of much hydroelectric power and its lower flood plains could become a major source of rice if flood control and irrigation projects begun by the French in the colonial
period are ever realized.

TOBACCO (Nicotiana tobacum). Successive development plans
have sought to achieve self-sufficiency in tobacco
which is grown widely as a subsistence crop throughout much of Guinea. Before independence there was
a private French tobacco estate near Nzérékoré and
the French tobacco monopoly had a tenant estate near
Beyla. To supply the cigarette factory built by the
People's Republic of China at Wassa-Wassa in 1966,
tobacco continues to be imported since Guinean production has diminished to practically nothing since independence.

TOMA (Loma). An ethnic group living to the east of the
Kissi in the Macenta administrative region. Unrelated
to their Kissi neighbors they probably represent an
early incursion of savanna peoples into the forest zone
some five hundred years ago. In Guinea they are
gradually being assimilated into the larger Maninka
populations.

TOUGUE. A town and region in the Futa Jalon between Dinguiraye and Labé on the border of the Republic of Mali.
The region has some bauxite deposits and 7000 acres
of plains suitable for mechanized rice cultivation. Currently it remains a relatively non-urban and non-in-
dustrialized region.

TOURE, AHMED SEKOU. The president since 1958 of the
Republic of Guinea, Sékou Touré was born January 9,
1922, at Faranah. Expelled from Georges Poiret Teacher's College after one year in 1937, Touré became
involved in union activity while serving as a clerk,
first with the Niger Francais, then with the colonial

Post Office and finally with the colonial Treasury Department. After having taken part in the organization
of the RDA in Bamako in 1946, he became a full-time
trade union official rising to importance not only in
Guinea but throughout AOF.

In 1952 Touré became secretary-general of
the Guinea branch of the RDA, was elected to the Territorial Assembly of Guinea in 1953 and became mayor of Conakry in 1958. In March 1957 he became
vice-president of the Government Council of Guinea.
In September 1957 he split with the RDA over separate
membership in the French Community and led Guinea
to a decisive vote for independence in the referendum
of September 28, 1958.

Touré has remained in office, in spite of
a series of coups and managerial errors, through repression and manipulation. Plots and counterplots
have become the hallmarks of his regime. Internally,
smuggling, profiteering and corruption have been a
constant challenge to the success of Touré's regime
while a certain paranoia has always plagued its foreign
relations.

A plot in January 1960 in which 19 death
sentences were handed out was partially blamed on
the French. Many French teachers and technicians
were expelled from Guinea at this time as was the
French Archbishop of Conakry. In October 1965 a
number of high officials were arrested and executed
following alleged French-backed anti-government activities. The "Labé Plot" linked to French imperialism was uncovered in February 1969. Following this,
Touré purged the army and ordered the execution of
13 people.

Though Touré has often been accused of
being a Soviet puppet by many Westerners his actions
do not seem to bear this out. During the so-called
"teacher's plot" of November 1961, Touré accused
Soviet Ambassador Daniel Solod of complicity and expelled him.

In 1962 Touré accused the Ghanaian government of ordering the assassination of Togo's President
Olympio on January 13 of that year. On March 2,
1966, he welcomed to Guinea the exiled President of
Ghana, Kwame Nkrumah, as his "co-President."

In 1963 widespread arrests and purging of
the PDG followed the "shopkeeper's plot." In April
1967 Touré ordered a wave of arrests to avert an al-

leged coup d'état and again purged the PDG in 1968.
Ministerial shake-up, impassioned harangues and constant purges of the party have followed almost yearly.
On June 24, 1969, Touré apparently narrow-
ly escaped an attempt on his life during a visit from
President Kenneth Kaunda of Zambia.  On November
2, 1970, dissident Guineans, mercenaries and Portuguese army elements failed in an attack on Conakry.
Following this, Sékou Touré ordered a "people's trial"
which condemned 92 to death.  In April 1971 while
visiting Medina another supposed attempt on his life
was uncovered.  Yet Touré remains in power, apparently supported by a large percentage of the Guinean
people.

TOURE, ISMAEL.  Three years younger than Sékou Touré,
Ismael Touré (the son of Sékou Touré's father's wife)
is Sékou's half-brother.  He was trained in France as
an electrician.  Returning to Guinea in 1950 he worked at the Kankan Weather Station where he was elected to the Municipal Council of Kankan and to the Territorial Assembly from Faranah in 1956.
Touré appointed him minister of public works
in his first cabinet.  He was successively minister of
posts, telegraphs and transport, of public works and
transport, of economic development, and of finance.
In June 1972 he was appointed minister of the Super
Ministry of Economy and Finance in charge of industry,
mining, power, banking, development and public works.
A self-contained and ambitious man, Ismael
Touré seems to have his brother's trust.  As long as
Sékou Touré retains power, Ismael Touré would seem
to have a place in the government.

TOURE, SAMORY.  Born about 1830 near Sanankoro, Guinea,
he became a trader at 17 and later served in the army
of a Maninka war leader.  By 1879 he had established
an independent state stretching from near Bamako,
Mali, to the Liberian forests and including Kankan,
the trading center of present-day Upper Guinea.  He
resisted the French from 1882 until his capture in 1898.
He ultimately died in exile in 1900 in Gabon.  Sékou
Touré claimed Samory Touré as an ancestor and used
the fact of Samory's resistance to the French and sense
of widespread unity for political purposes in the mid-
1950s.

TRADE--EXTERNAL. Guinea's export earnings throughout
the 1960s stagnated. Never recovering from the a-
brupt withdrawal of French price supports and technical expertise after independence, Guinean agriculture
continues to perform poorly. One-third of the coffee
crop, for example, is smuggled out since legal ex-
portation requires the surrender of foreign exchange
in return for overvalued Guinean currency which effectively reduces earnings by about three-fourths.
Guinean foreign debt exceeded $560 million in 1973
in spite of massive external capital infusions from
1959 on. Yet bauxite and alumina exports and the
potential of iron ore exports continue to give Guinea
some prospect of economic viability in the future.

TRADE--INTERNAL. Critical shortages of food and other
basic consumer products continued in the mid 1970s.
Illicit trade in soap, sugar, rice and cooking oils, at
three or four times the legal price, was rampant.
Smuggling was still widespread and many farmers produced only for family consumption rather than for a
cash market. Domestic trade remained in much the
same chaos that had followed the government's attempt
to control all trade in 1960. Trade in perishable
foodstuffs on a small scale continues between rural
areas and the towns but even this would appear to
have declined.

TRADE UNIONS. Much of the African political activity in
French Guinea from 1946 on was conducted within the
framework of the French Confédération Générale du
Travail (CGT). The iron and bauxite mines of Lower
Guinea became fertile recruiting grounds for union organization by the early 1950s. After the 66-day strike
in the fall of 1953, union membership in Guinea rose
from 4,600 before the strike to 44,000 in 1955. Since
Sékou Touré was the secretary-general of the CGT and
most of its leaders, like him, were loyal members of
the Parti Démocratique de Guinée, the politization of
the CGT in Guinea was almost total by January 1957,
when Touré broke with this French Communist union
and created the autonomous Union Générale des Travailleurs Afrique Noire (UGTAN). By then the political base afforded by the union had helped Touré be
elected to the French National Assembly and the union
had outlived its political usefulness. See CONFEDERA-
TION GENERALE DU TRAVAIL; UNION GENERAL DES
TRAVAILLEURS D'AFRIQUE NOIRE.

TRANSPORTATION. Like most West African countries, Guinea suffers from an inadequate transportation infrastructure. The country has only about 28,400 kilometers of roads of any sort and less than 12,400 of these are practical for ordinary vehicular traffic. Outside the capital, perhaps 520 kilometers are hard surfaced. The railroad from Conakry to Fria and the 135-kilometer heavygauge line from the Boké bauxite deposits to the new deep-water port at Kamsar are in good condition but the antiquated narrow gauge line from Conakry to Kankan is hardly functioning beyond Kindia. The Guinean airline, Air Guinée (q. v.), functions at a loss on an irregular schedule while the port facilities at Conakry are badly in need of better managerial and technical direction.

TRAORE, MAMADOU see RAY, AUTRA

TSETSE FLIES. A dark-brown or yellowish-brown fly about the size of a large housefly with projecting proboscis which carries sleeping sickness to humans and domestic animals. Found more commonly in northeastern Guinea they are one of the reasons for the relatively sparse populations in some areas of Upper Guinea.

TYAPI (or Tiapi) see LANDOUMA


-U-


UNION GENERALE DES TRAVAILLEURS D'AFRIQUE NOIRE (UGTAN). Interterritorial trade movement founded in Cotonou, People's Republic of Benin (then Dahomey), in January 1957 in an attempt to create an autonomous African trade union movement free of French or other European trade union control. Headed by Sékou Touré, UGTAN split at the 1959 Congress in Conakry and for all practical purposes ceased to function. The Confédération Nationale des Travailleurs de Guinée continued on as a separate Guinean organization.

UNITED NATIONS. Guinea became the 82nd member of the United Nations in December 1958. Throughout the sixties it played a leadership role among African and "Third World" nations at the UN. Guinea sent a 749-man battalion to the Congo as part of the UN peacekeeping force there in 1960. Guinea has ceased play-

ing such an important role in the General Assembly
in recent years though the country still raises its
voice occasionally over anti-colonial and African is-
sues of immediate concern to its own interests. Though
Guinea belongs to most of the UN's specialized agencies, it receives mission of the World Health Organization, UNESCO, and other agencies with so many restrictions that they seldom are able to offer much
assistance to the country. Guinea is voluntarily ex-
cluded from the General Agreement on Tariffs and
Trade, for example, as it tries to maintain its economic isolation.

UPPER GUINEA. One of the four reasonably clearly marked
    topographical areas into which Guinea is divided. This
    eastern portion of the country is an extension of the
    Futa Jalon (q. v. ) shading off into the basin of the Up-
    per Niger in a classical orchard shrub and grassland
    savanna.

URBANIZATION. With around 200,000 inhabitants, the cap-
    ital of Guinea, Conakry, is the country's only real
    urban center. The old city on Tumbo Island retains
    its colonial facade. To this is joined a Kaloum
    Peninsula community which has grown up in the past
    twenty years. From the tip of the peninsula to San-
    oya 35 kilometers away is an industrial zone with a
    growing salaried urbanized population giving Greater
    Conakry a population in excess of 500,000.
            The second largest town, Kankan, in Upper
    Guinea, has perhaps 40,000 inhabitants but it is more
    a large cluster of Maninka villages around an admin-
    istrative and commercial core area than a truly ur-
    ban area. Most other towns throughout Guinea follow
    basically the same pattern.
            Boké and Fria, with their mining complexes
    are isolated outposts of what would seem to be trans-
    planted towns deposited in Guinea from somewhere
    else. The highrise apartments, tennis courts, swim-
    ming pools and company commissaries for the European
    community connected with the bauxite works in these
    towns have little impact on the lives of most Guineans.

-V-

VICTOIRE DE 27 DECEMBRE. Refers to the election of De-

cember 27, 1974, in which President Touré was over-
whelmingly re-elected for the third time by popular
election. (His first election had been by the National
Assembly in 1958.) This election was made possible
by a constitutional amendment which allowed unlimited
re-election in place of the previous limit of two pre-
sidential terms in office.

VOIX DE LA REVOLUTION. This is the usual identification
of Guinea's single government-owned radio station
which is also occasionally identified as Radiodiffusion
Nationale or Radiodiffusion de la République de Guinée.
Transmission is from Conakry in both shortwave and
mediumwave at between 10 and 100 kilowatts for 12
to 24 hours a day. Since the country has between
100,000 and 125,000 radio receivers it is estimated
that more than 50 percent of the population receive
the broadcasts. These broadcasts consist of extensive coverage of the activities and speeches of President Touré, various party and governmental events,
news in both French and Guinean vernaculars, and
African music and songs.


-W-

WAHHABIYA. A Muslim community or brotherhood (see
Qadiriya and Tijaniya) founded by Muhammed ibn abd
al Wahhab in Arabia in the 18th century. Wahhabis
strive to live simple lives, following the strict rule
of the early followers of the Prophet Muhammed, and
avoiding changes and compromises of later Islamic
teaching. Never very widespread in Guinea, this
brotherhood was represented in Guinea by a few re-
formist Maninka Muslim teachers in Kankan in the
1950s.

WATERWAYS. Few of Guinea's coastal rivers are navigable
for more than a short distance inland. The Niger
was navigable by river steamer from Kouroussa to
Bamako, Mali in July and August until the steamer
ceased functioning in 1948. Shallow draft boats and
barges still made the trip into the 1960s, in some
years from July to November depending on the quan-
tity of rain received. The Milo, the Niger's largest
southern tributary, also carried such traffic as far
south as Kankan until the decline in commercial traf-

fic with Mali made these routes unnecessary.

WILLIAM PONTY SCHOOL. The principal secondary school
established by the French in West Africa. Located
in Dakar, Senegal, this school trained African clerks,
teachers and medical assistants, free of charge, for
service to the colonial regime between 1918 and 1945.
The vast majority of post-1945 African political activists throughout most of French West Africa were
graduates of this school. In Guinea the Ponty graduates were mostly Fulbê from wealthy families of the
Futa Jalon and never overcame their rather exclusive
ethnic origins in order to appeal to all Guineans. The
majority of the trade union leadership among whom
Sékou Touré derived early support were not Ponty
graduates though. In fact, a certain hostility to Ponty
graduates underlines much of Touré's actions in the
1950s and 1960s.

WOMEN. Within most traditional social systems of Guinea,
women were often placed in a subordinate position.
To a large extent these roles have been changed since
independence through the efforts of the party and its
auxillary, the Comité National des Femmes (q. v.).
Traditional marriage practices have been changed
greatly. Civil marriage is now compulsory and a
minimum marriage age of 17 for women has been
fixed. Bride wealth has been reduced to a symbolic
sum payable to the woman herself in front of a civil
authority. Polygamy has been outlawed in theory since
1968 though this law is not universally enforced. The
percentage of girls in school has risen from 4 percent
in 1958 to over 20 percent. Women's cooperatives in
sewing, dying, embroidery and other crafts have been
given government support. Finally all professions
are open to women and there are women in the army,
militia, police and administration. The ideal of total
equality between men and women has been theoretically
established in Guinea and in this predominantly Muslim
society the changes in the years since independence
have been quite remarkable.

WORLD WAR II. For the majority of Guineans the early
years of the war represented a period of extreme
hardship. The worst forms of racism and colonial
oppression were openly practiced under the Vichy regime. Pressed into labor service on European planta-

tions and government construction projects, forced to
sell agricultural goods below market price, and sub-
jected to shortages of basic commodities, Guineans
suffered greatly.   Not until well into 1943 did the Free
French begin to govern throughout Guinea.   Even then
Guineans were forced to produce labor for a cause
which was of very little direct importance to them.
Production did rise and some small-scale industrialization was begun in Guinea during the war, but for
the most part the Allied victory in 1945 was the oc-
casion for little rejoicing for Guineans.


-Y-

YEYE MUSIC.   French style popular music which was banned
by the JRDA at its sixth Congress held in 1971.   This
is part of a continuing effort by the PDG to return to
African musical sources and part of the total cultural
revolution being attempted in all aspects of Guinean
life.

YOUKOUNKOUN.   Renamed Koundora (q. v. ).

YOUMOU.   A small administrative region created in the early
1970s located on the Liberian border south of Macenta
and Nzérékoré.   On the Liberian frontier this region
is carefully watched as a smuggling outlet for the coffee grown in the Forest zone.


-Z-

ZIAMA FOREST.   A reserve of primary forest in the Macenta region (q. v. ) which has been reserved for exploitation by keeping out the local cultivators.   In the
late 1960s a concession of 250,000 acres in this forest was to ship timber to the sawmill at Nzérékoré
(q. v. ).   The poorly maintained mountain roads made
this 65-mile trip impractical and the forest has contributed little to Guinean forestry industries.

# BIBLIOGRAPHY

## Introductory Essay

There are only a handful of really original books dealing with Guinea. Perhaps the best of the general works is Jean Suret-Canale's République de Guinée (1970), strong on socioeconomic development but weak on political aspects of Guinea. Charles Rivière's Guinea (1977) is an up-to-date source in English which supersedes his Mutations Sociales en Guinée (1971). 'Lapido Adamolekun's Sékou Touré's Guinea (1976) was the first comprehensive analysis in English of political, social and economic developments in post independence Guinea. Though somewhat naive in his analysis of Guinea's success in nation building, Adamolekun's work is still valuable. The latest Area Handbook for Guinea (1975) also provides relatively accurate data on the social, political and economic aspects of Guinea society. This work is largely the result of research in secondary sources and lacks the insight which two study visits to Guinea in 1968 and 1970-71 give to Adamolekun's work.

Since Guinea never played as large a role as Senegal or the Ivory Coast in the history of French West Africa bibliographic citations from the pre-independence period are relatively infrequent. But Guinea was the second Black African nation to achieve its independence from European colonial rule in the 20th century. When the people of Guinea rejected de Gaulle's proposed Franco-African community by an overwhelming no vote in the September 28, 1958 referendum the country was suddenly thrust into the limelight of international affairs. For a time there was a large, if uneven, outpouring of literature on Guinea. A number of popular books appeared in the U.S. during this period. For example, William Attwood's The Reds and the Blacks (1967), and John H. Morrow's First American Ambassador to Guinea (1968), represent two such popular works with a sympathetic, though Amero-Centric view.

Guinea's first president, Sékou Touré, was much written about as an international figure. His outspoken anti-colonial positions and his views on African Socialism continued to attract the attention of the academic community throughout the 1960s in such works as W. A. E. Skurnick's African Political Thought (1968) and Gwendolyn M. Carter's African One Party States (1962).

With the Portuguese-backed commando raid on Guinea on November 21, 1970, the strain of extreme isolationism which had always been present at times of internal political crisis became dominant in Guinean affairs. Contemporary materials on Guinea suffer from the difficulties always present under totalitarian regimes. The foreign press and the more than a million Guinea living outside the country often present a rather unflattering view of conditions within the country. The rise of Touré himself as the sole interpreter of national realities since 1970 (see Sékou Touré Le Chemin du Socialisme, 1970) has stifled most information emanating from within Guinea. Guinea, to paraphrase the Eurocentric and racist viewpoints held about all of Africa until recently, has again become part of the "Dark Continent." The 24-hour-a-day broadcasts by radio Conakry, Voix de la Révolution, casts little light on contemporary affairs. Readers should remain alert, then, for the uneven and subjective nature of much of the literature on Guinea since independence.

## Abbreviations in the Bibliography

| | |
|---|---|
| A. G. | Annales de Géographie |
| Bull. C. E. H. S. | Bulletin du Comité d'Etudes Historiques et Scientifiques de l'A. O. F. |
| Bull. I. F. A. N. | Bulletin de l'Institut Français d'Afrique Noire |
| Bull. et Mém. Soc. anthropologie | Bulletin et Mémoires Sociétés d'Anthropologie |
| Cahiers d'I. S. E. A. | Cahiers de l'Institut de Science Economique Appliquée |
| C. E. A. | Cahiers d'Etudes Africaines |
| C. O. M. | Cahiers d'Outre-mer |

| | |
|---|---|
| C. R. A. S. | Comptes Rendus des Séances de l'Aca-démie des Sciences |
| C. R. S. S. G. F. | Comptes Rendus des Séances de la Société Géologique de France |
| E. G. | Etudes Guinéennes |
| E. S. A. | Ecole Supérieure d'Administration |
| I. F. A. N. | Institut Français d'Afrique Noire |
| I. N. R. D. G. | Imprimerie Nationale de République de Guinée |
| I. P. C. | Institut Polytechnique Gamal Abdel Nasser de Conakry |
| J. A. H. | Journal of African History |
| J. A. T. B. A. | Journal d'Agronomie Tropicale et de Botanique Appliquée |
| J. S. A. | Journal de la Société des Africanists |
| mech. dup. | mechanically duplicated |
| ms. | manuscript or typescript |
| n. d. | no date |
| O. R. S. T. O. M. | Office de la Recherche Scientifique et Technique Outre-Mer |
| P. A. | Présence Africaine |
| P. U. F. | Presses Universitaires de France |
| R. A. | Recherches Africaines |
| R. F. E. P. A. | Revue Française d'Etudes Politiques Africaines |
| R. D. G. | Revue de Géomorphologie Dynamique |
| R. J. P. U. F. | Revue Juridique et Politique de l'Union Française |

## A Note on the Scope

　　　　The books and articles in this bibliography are mainly chosen from those available in English and French. A few Russian, German and Portuguese languages sources are also noted. All of the citations are organized under the following broad subject headings, each of which is further divided into two or more of these four categories: books, articles, government documents, and dissertations; at the end of section 14 are maps.

1   General Works

2   Early Historical and Exploration Accounts

3   Historical Studies

4   Anthropology, Ethnology and Sociology

5   Contemporary Politics

6   Economics

7   Education

8   Scientific Studies

9   Religion

10  Literature and Poetry

11  Linguistics

12  Art and Music

13  Tourism

14  Reference and Bibliography

# 1 GENERAL WORKS

## BOOKS

Adamolekun, 'Ladipo. Sékou Touré's Guinea. London: Methuen, 1976.

Afrique occidentale française. 2 vols. Paris: Encyclopédie Coloniale et Maritime, 1949.

Ajayi, J. F. Ade, and Crowder, Michael (eds.). History of West Africa, I. London: Longman, 1971.

_____. History of West Africa, II. London: Longman, 1974.

Ameillon, B. La Guinée: bilan d'une independance. Paris: F. Maspero, 1964.

Autra, Ray (Mamadou Traoré). Connaissance de la République de Guinée. Dakar: A. Diop, 1960.

Charles, Bernard. Guinée. Lausanne: Editions Rencontre, 1963.

_____. La Republique de Guinée. Paris: Berger-Levrault 1972.

Church, R. J. Harrison. West Africa, 6th ed. New York: John Wiley and Sons, 1968.

Decouflé, A. Sociologie des révolutions. Paris: P. U. F., 1968.

Diagne, Peter. Pouvoir politique tradionnel en Afrique occidentale. Paris: P. A., 1967.

Fage, J. D. An Atlas of African History. London: Edward Arnold, 1958.

_____. A History of West Africa: An Introductory Survey. Cambridge, England: Cambridge University Press, 1969.

Gigon, Fernand. Guinée, Etat-Pilote. Paris: Plon, 1959.

Hapgood, David. Africa: From Independence to Tomorrow. New York: Atheneum, 1965.

Hardy, George. Histoire de la colonisation française. Paris: Larose, 1953.

_____. Histoire sociale de la colonisation française. Paris: Larose, 1953.

_____. La Politique coloniale et le partage de la terre aux XIX$^e$+XX$^e$ siècles. Paris: Albin Michel, 1937.

Houis, M. La Guinée française. Editions maritimes et coloniales. Paris: 1953.

Legum, Colin, and Drysdale, John (eds.). African Contemporary Record: Annual Survey and Documents. 1968-1969, I. London: Africa Research, 1969.

_____ and _____ (eds.). _____, 1969-1970, II. Exeter: Africa Research, 1970.

_____ (ed.). _____, 1970-71, III. London: Rex Collings, 1971.

_____ (ed.). _____, 1971-72, IV; 1972-1973, V; 1973-1974, VI; 1974-1975, VII; 1975-1976, VIII. New York: Africana Publishing, 1972; 1973; 1974; 1975; 1976.

Milcent, Ernest. L'A.O.F. entre en scène. Paris: Editions Témoignage Chrétien, 1958.

Morgan, W.B., and Pugh, J.C. West Africa. London: Methuen, 1969.

Nelson, Harold C., et al. Area Handbook for Guinea. Washington, D.C.: U.S. Gov. Printing Office, 1975.

Paulme, Denise. Les Civilisations africaines. Paris: P.U.F., 1959.

Pedler, E.J. Economic Geography of West Africa. London: Longmans, Green, 1955.

Priestly, Herbert Inghram.  France Overseas:  A Study of
    Modern Imperialism.  New York:  Appleton-Century,
    1938.

Richard-Molard, Jacques.  Afrique occidentale française.
    Paris:  Berger-Levrault, 1949.

Rivière,Claude.  Guinea.  Ithaca, N. Y. :  Cornell University
    Press, 1977.

Suret-Canale, Jean.  Afrique noire:  occidentale et centrale,
    I.  Paris:  Editions Sociales, 1964.

_____.  Afrique noire:  occidentale et centrale, II.  Pa-
    ris:  Editions Sociales, 1968.

_____.  La Republique de Guinée.  Paris:  Editions So-
    ciales, 1970.

_____, and Niane, Djibril Tamsir.  Histoire de l'Afrique
    occidentale.  Paris:  P. A. , 1961.

Thompson, Virginia, and Adloff, Richard.  French West Af-
    rica.  Stanford, Calif. :  Stanford University Press,
    1958.

Voss, Joachim.  Guinea.  Bonn:  Schroeder, 1968.


ARTICLES

Balandier, G.  "Les Etudes guinéennes, "  E. G.  1 (1947),
    pp. 5-6.

Cowan, L. Gray.  "Guinea, "  in African One-Party States,
    Gwendolen M. Carter, ed. Ithaca:  Cornell University
    Press, 1962, pp. 149-236.

"Dossier Guinée, "  Remarques Africaines, XIII, No. 388
    (November 25, 1971), pp. 414-419.

"Guinea, "  Africa South of the Sahara, 1974 (1976), pp. 388-401.

Henderson, Gregory.  "Guinea, "  in Public Diplomacy and Po-
    litical Change:  Four Case Studies, Gregory Hender-
    son, ed. New York:  Praeger, 1973, pp. 317-339.

"Isolation of Guinea Makes Assessment of Nation Difficult,"
Le Monde (October 3, 1973), 1.


2 EARLY HISTORICAL AND EXPLORATION ACCOUNTS


BOOKS

Alexander, James E.  Narrative of a Voyage of Observation
Among the Colonies of Western Africa. 2 vols. London: H. Colburn, 1837.

Astley, Thomas.  A New General Collection of Voyages and
Travels. 4 vols. London: 1745.

Barbot, Jean.  Description of the Coasts of North and South
Guinea. London: Henry Linto, 1732.

Blagdon, Francis.  Modern Discoveries.  London: J. Ridge-
way, 1803.

Ca Da Mosto, Alvise de.  Relation des voyages à la côté
occidentale d'Afrique.  Paris: E. Leroux, 1895.

Fernandez, V.  Description de la côté occidentale d'Afrique
(du Sénégal au cap de Monte), translated and notes by
Th. Monod, A. Teixeira da Mota and R. Mauny. Bissau: Centro de estudos da Guiné portuguesa, 1951.

Gray, Major William, and Dochard, Staff Surgeon.  Travels
in Western Africa in the Years 1819-1821 from the
River Gambia, through Woolli, Bondoo, Galam, Kassan,
Kaarta, and Foolidoo to the River Niger.  London:
Murray, 1825.

Labat, Jean Baptiste.  Nouvelle relation de l'Afrique occidentale. 5 vols. Paris: Cavalier, 1782.

Laing, Gordon.  Voyage dans le Timanni, le Kouranko et le
Soulimana.  Paris: Delaforest et Arthus-Bertrand,
1826.

Le Maire, Jacques-Joseph.  Voyage to the Canaries, Cape
Verdo and the Coast of Africa under the Command of
M. Dancourt, 1682, translated by Edmund Goldsmid.
Edinburgh: 1887. (private printing).

Madrolle, Claudius.  En Guinée.  Paris:  Le 'Soudier, 1895.

Matthews, John.  A Voyage to the River Sierra Leone, translated by Bellart.  London:  B. White and Son and T.
Sewell, 1788.

Mollien, Gaspard.  Travels in the Interior of Africa to the
Senegal and Gambia in the Year 1818, ed. T. E. Bow-
dich.  London:  Phillips, 1820.

Monod, Theodore, Teixeira da Mota, A. and Mauny, R. (eds.).
Description de la Côte Occidentale d'Afrique par Va-
lentin Fernandes (1506-1510).  Bissau:  Centro de estudos da Guiné portuguesa, 1938.

Noirot, E.  A travers le Fouta-Djalon et le Bambouk.  Paris:  Dreyfus, 1885.

Pacheco Pereira, Duarte.  Esmeraldo de Situ Orbis.  Bissau:  Centro de estudos da Guiné portuguesa, 1956.

Park, Mungo.  Journal of a Mission to the Interior of Africa
in the Year 1805.  London:  Bulmer, 1815.

_____.  Travels in the Interior Districts of Africa.  Lon-
don:  Bulmer, 1799.

Rançon, A.  Dans la Haute-Gambie.  Voyage d'exploration
scientifique, 1891-1892.  Paris:  Société d'Editions
Scientifiques, 1894.

Sanderval, O. de.  La Conquête du Fouta-Djalon.  Paris:
Challamel, 1899.

Smith, William.  A New Voyage to Guinea.  London:  J.
Nourse, 1744.

Walckenaer, Charles Athanase.  Nouvelle histoire générale
des voyages; ou collection des relations de voyages
par mer et par terre.  Paris:  Chez Lefèvre, 1826.

Whitford, John.  Trading Life in Western and Central Africa.  London:  1877.

Zurara, Gomès Eanès de.  Chronique de Guinée.  Dakar:
I. F. A. N. , 1960.

## ARTICLES

Gouldsbury, Dr. "Englische Expedition unter Dr. Gouldsbury nach dem oberem Gambia und Futa-Djallon," Petermann's Mitteilungen, XXVIII (1882), pp. 290-296.

Lambert, M. "Voyage dans le Fouta-Djalon," Le Tour du monde (1861), pp. 373-400.

Vieillard, G. "Notes sur l'exode toucouleur," C. E. A., I (1960), pp. 193-197.

## 3 HISTORICAL STUDIES

### BOOKS

Amin, Samir. L'Afrique de l'ouest bloquée: l'économie politique de la colonisation, 1880-1970. Paris: Editions de Minuit, 1971.

Arcin, André. La Guinée française. Paris: Challamel, 1911.

_____. Histoire de la Guinée française. Paris: Challamel, 1907.

Aspe-Fleurimont. La Guinée française. Paris: Challamel, 1900.

Betts, Raymond F. Assimilation and Association in French Colonial Theory, 1890-1914. New York: Columbia University Press, 1961.

Blanchet, André. L'Itinéraire des partis africains depuis Bamako. Paris: Plon, 1958.

Borella, F. L'Evolution politique et juridique de l'Union Française depuis 1946. Paris: R. Pichon & R. Durand-Auzias, 1958.

Chailley, Marcel. Histoire de l'Afrique occidentale française. Paris: Berger-Levrault, 1968.

Cohen, William B. Rulers of Empire: The French Colonial

Service in Africa. Stanford, Calif., Hoover Institution
Press, Stanford University, 1971.

Corbett, Edward M. The French Presence in Black Africa.
Washington, D. C.: Black Orpheus Press, 1972.

Cornevin, Robert. Histoire de l'Afrique des origines nos
jours. Paris: Payot, 1956.

_____. Histoire des peuples de l'Afrique noire. Paris:
Berger-Levrault, 1960.

Davidson, Basil. A History of West Africa to the Nineteenth-
Century. Garden City: Doubleday, 1966.

Davies, Oliver. West Africa Before the Europeans: Archae-
ology and Prehistory. London: Methuen, 1967.

Delavignett, Robert. Freedom and Authority in French West
Africa. New York: Oxford University Press, 1957.

Deloncle, Pierre. L'Afrique occidentale française: découverte, pacification, mise en valeur. Paris: Editions
Ernest Leroux, 1934.

Demougeot, A. Notes sur l'organisation politique et administrative du Labê avant et depuis l'occupation française.
Paris: Larousse, 1944.

Deschamps, Hubert J. Afrique noire prê-coloniale. Paris:
P. U. F., 1962.

_____. Les Méthodes et doctrines de colonisation de la
France. Paris: Armand Colin, 1953.

_____. Les Religions de l'Afrique noire. Paris: P. U. F.,
1960.

D'Horel, P. Afrique occidentale: Sénégal, Guinée, Côte
d'Ivoire, Dahomey. Paris: 1905.

Du Bois, Victor D. Guinea: The Years Before World War
II. New York: American Universities Field Staff,
Reports service, West Africa Series, vol. V, no. 5,
1962.

_____. The Guinean Vote for Independence: The Maneuv-

ering Before the Referendum of September 28, 1958.
New York: American Universities Field Staff Reports,
West Africa Series, Guinea, V, No. 7, 1962.

_____. Guinea's Prelude to Independence: Political Ac-
tivity, 1945-58. New York: American Universities
Field Staff Reports, West Africa Series, Guinea, V,
No. 6, 1962.

Duchène, Albert. La Politique coloniale de la France. Paris: Payot, 1928.

Famechan, M. Notice sur la Guinée française. Paris: Al-
can-Lévy, 1900.

Galéma, Guilavogui. La Résistance à la pénétration française
dans la région de Macenta. Conakry: I. P. C., 1968.

Gifford, Prosser, and Louis, William Roger (eds.). France
and Britain in Africa: Imperial Rivalry and Colonial
Rule. New Haven: Yale University Press, 1971.

Gorges, E. H. The Great War in West Africa. London:
Hutchinson, 1927.

Guinée, prélude à l'indépendance. Paris: P. A., 1959.

Hargreaves, John D. Prelude to the Partition of West Africa. New York: St. Martin's Press, 1966.

_____. West Africa: The Former French States. Engle-
wood Cliffs, N. J.: Prentice-Hall, 1967.

Harmand, Jules. Domination et colonisation. Paris: Payot,
1940.

Histoire et épopée des troupes coloniales. Paris: Presse
Moderne, 1956.

Holt, P. M., Lambton, Ann K. S., and Lewis, Bernard (eds.).
The Cambridge History of Islam: Volume II, The Further Islamic Lands, Islamic Society and Civilization.
Cambridge, England: Cambridge University Press,
1970.

Ingold, Commandant François. Les Troupes noires au combat. Paris: Berger-Levrault, 1940.

Levtzion, Nehemia. Ancient Ghana and Mali. Studies in
     African History, No. 7. London: Methuen, 1973.

Machat, J. Guinée française: les riviéres du sud et le
     Fouta-Djalon. Paris: Challamel, 1906.

Martin, Gaston. Histoire de l'esclavage dans les colonies
     françaises. Paris: P. U. F. , 1948.

Morrow, John H. First American Ambassador to Guinea.
     New Brunswick, N. J. : Rutgers University Press,
     1968.

Mortimer, Edward. France and the Africans, 1944-1960:
     A Political History. New York: Walker, 1969.

Neres, Philip. French-Speaking West Africa: From Colon-
     ial Status to Independence. London: Oxford University
     Press, 1962.

Niane, Djibril Tamsir. Recherches sur L'Empire du Mali
     au Moyen Age, No. 2. Conakry: Institut National
     de Recherches et de Documentation, 1962.

_____, and Suret-Canale, Jean. Histoire de l'Afrique oc-
     cidentale, Conakry, Ministère de l'Education nationale.
     Conakry: I. N. R. D. G. , 1960.

Oliver, Roland, and Fage, J. D. A Short History of Africa.
     Baltimore: Penguin Books, 1962.

Panikkar, Kavalan Madhusudan. Revolution in Africa. Bom-
     bay: Asia Publishing House, 1961.

Person, Yves. Samori. Une révolution dyula, Vol. 1. Nî-
     mes: Barnier, 1968.

Pré, Roland. L'Avenir de la Guinée française. Conakry:
     Editions guinéennes, 1951.

Robert, Andre P. L'Evolution des coutumes de l'ouest af-
     ricain et la législation française. Paris: Encyclo-
     pédie d'Outre-mer, 1955.

Roberts, Stephen H. History of French Colonial Policy
     (1870-1925), I. London: P. S. King, 1929. Reprint-
     ed London: Frank Cass, 1963.

Rouget, F. La Guinée. Corbeil: Crété, 1906.

Santos, Anani. L'Option des indigènes en faveur de l'application de la loi française (en A. O. F. et au Togo). Paris: Maurice Lavergne, 1943.

Saurrat, Albert. La Mise en valeur des colonies françaises. Paris: Payot, 1923.

Schnapper, Bernard. La Politique et le commerce français dans le golfe de Guinée de 1838 à 1871. Paris: Mouton, 1961.

Stride, G. T. , and Ifeka, Caroline. Peoples and Empires of West Africa: West Africa in History, 1000-1800. New York: Africana Publishing, 1971.

Suret-Canale, Jean. L'Ere coloniale. Paris: Editions Sociales, 1964.

_____. French Colonialism in Tropical Africa, 1900-1945, translated by Till Gottheiner. New York: Pica Press 1971.

Teixeira da Mota, A. Inquérito etnográfico. Bissau: 1947.

Webster, J. B. , and Boahen, A. A. History of West Africa: The Revolutionary Years--1815 to Independence. New York: Praeger, 1970.

Weygand, Général Maxime. Histoire de l'armée française. Paris: Flammarian, 1953.

ARTICLES

Allainment, Y. "Note sur l'identification des tombes de Campbell et Peddie à Boké (Guinée)," Bull. I. F. A. N., 3 (1941), pp. 74-78.

Arlabosse, General. "Une Phase de la lutte contre Samory 1890-1892," Revue de l'histoire des colonies françaises, 25 (1932), pp. 385-432, 465-514.

Attwood, William, and Loeb, James I. "Africa and Acts of Dissent," Washington Post, (December 12, 1971), p. 21.

Autra, Ray (Mamadou Traoré). "La République de Guinée...
    en bref," R. A. (1959), pp. 7-17.

Baillaud, E. "Observations and reflections on European ag-
    riculture in Guinea," Journal of the African Society,
    6 (1907), pp. 267-280.

Brière, D. "Souvenirs guinéens. Les Débuts du Cercle de
    Télimélé," E. G. , 8 (1952), pp. 3-12.

Chaleur, O. "La Guinée après trois ans d'indépendance,"
    Etudes (November, 1961), pp. 202-215.

Colombier, Th. du. "Une Expédition franco-belge en Guinée,"
    Bulletin Société belge d'études coloniales (May-June,
    1920), pp. 43 ff.

Crespin, M. "Alpha Yaya et M. Frézouls," Revue indigène,
    no. 2 (1906), pp. 45-46.

Cruise O'Brien, Donal. "Guinea, Recent history," Africa
    South of the Sahara, 1974 (1974), pp. 377-378.

Davidson, Basil. "Guinea: Past and Present," History
    Today, IX, No. 6 (June, 1959), pp. 392-398.

Demougeot, A. "Histoire du Nunez," Bull. C. E. H. S. , XXI
    (1938), pp. 177-289.

Diallo, Ousmane. "Connaissance historique de la Guinée,"
    P. A. , XXIX (December, 1959-January, 1960), pp.
    45-52.

_____. "Evolution sociale chez les Peuls du Fouta-Dja-
    lon," R. A. (October-December, 1961), pp. 73-94.

Fillot, Henri. "Alpha Yaya et M. Frézouls," Revue indi-
    gène, no. 4 (1906), pp. 85-88.

Fisher, G. "Quelques Aspects de la doctrine politique gui-
    néenne," Civilisations, 9 (1959), pp. 457-476.

Gaillard, M. "Niani, ancienne capitale de l'Empire mandin-
    gue," Bull. C. E. H. S. , no. 4, (1923), pp. 620-636.

Halle, C. "Notes sur Koly Tenguella, Olivier de Sanderval
    et les ruines de Gueme-Sangan," R. A. , 1 (1960),

Harris, Joseph E. "Protest and Resistance to the French in Fouta Diallon," Genève-Afrique, VIII (1969), pp. 3-18.

Hughes, John. "Communist Focus on Guinea," New Leader, XLII (July 6, 1959), pp. 3-4.

Humblot, P. "Kankan, métropole de la Haute-Guinée," Afrique française, renseignements coloniaux (1921), no. 6, pp. 129-141 and no. 7, pp. 153-163.

_____. "Origine et légende de Kankan et du Baté," La Guinée française (June 15, 1950).

"In memoriam: Monseigneur Lerouge, premier Evêque de Guinée, n'est plus," E. G. , 4 (1950), p. 81.

"Independent Guinea," P. A. , Special No. (1960).

Maguet, E. "La Condition juridique des terres en Guinée française," Afrique française, renseignements coloniaux, no. 3 (1926), pp. 121-126.

Maigret, J. "A la recherche du temps perdu," E. G. , I (1947), pp. 7-8.

Mangolte, Jacques. "Le Chemin de fer de Konakry au Niger (1890-1914)," Revue française d'histoire d'outre-mer, LV (1968), pp. 37-105.

Maupoil, B. "Notes concernant l'histoire des Coniagui-Bassari et en particulier l'occupation de leur pays par les Français," Bull. I. F. A. N. , XVI-B (1954), pp. 378-389.

Monod, Th. "Introduction [sur Richard-Molard]," R. A. , 4 (1961), pp. 6-7.

Newbury, C. W. "The Formation of the Government General of French West Africa," J. A. H. , no. 1 (1960), pp. 11-128.

Niane, Djibril Tamsir. "A propos de Koli Tenguella," R. A. , 4 (1960), pp. 33-36.

_____. "Soundjata ou l'épopée mandingue," P. A. (1960).

Ousmane, D. "Connaissance historique de la Guinée,"

P. A. , 29 (1959-1960), pp. 45-52.

Person, Y.   "La Jeunesse de Samori," Revue française d'histoire d'outre-mer, 49 (1962), pp. 151-180.

Portères, Roland.  "Vieilles Agricultures de l'Afrique intertropicale," Agronomie tropicale, nos. 9-10 (1950), pp. 489-507.

Poujade, J.   "La Guinée est-elle le dernier jalon d'un ancien Empire? Nos méthodes de travail," E. G. , 2 (1947), pp. 3-7.

Quinquaud, J.   "La Pacification du Fouta-Djalon," Revue d'histoire des colonies, 4$^e$ trim. (1938), pp. 49-134.

Richard-Molard, J.   "Découverte de la Guinée. Extraits d'un carnet de route," R. A. , 4 (1961), pp. 8-23.

Rivière, Claude.   "Le Long des côtes de Guinée avant la phase coloniale," Bull. I. F. A. N. , XXX-B, 2 (1968), pp. 727-750.

Robinson, Kenneth.   "Constitutional Reform in French Tropical Africa," Political Studies, vol. 6 (February, 1958), pp. 45-69.

_____ .   "The Public Law of Overseas France Since the War," The Journal of Comparative Legislation, XXXII (1950).

Rudin, Harry R.   "Guinea Outside the French Community," Current History, XXXVII, (July, 1959), pp. 13-16.

Soubbotine, V. A.   "Du régime foncier au Fouta-Djalon avant la colonisation," Congrès international des sciences anthropologiques et ethnologiques, VIIe (August, 1964).

Suret-Canale, J.   "A propos du Ovali de Goumba," R. A. (1964), pp. 160-164.

_____ .   "L'Almamy Samory Toure," R. A. , 1-4 (1959), pp. 18-22.

_____ .   "Essai sur la signification historique et sociale des hégémonies peules," Cahiers du C. E. R. M. (1964). Mech. dup.

_____. "La Fin de la chefferie en Guinée," J. A. H. , VII (1966), pp. 459-493.

_____. "La Guinée dans le système colonial," P. A. , XXIX (December, 1959-January, 1960), pp. 9-44.

_____. "Le Siège de Boussédou (février-avril 1907)," R. A. (1964), pp. 165-166.

Teixeira da Mota, A. "Nota sobre a historia dos Fulas. Coli Tenguéla e a chegada dos primeiros Fulas aô Futa-Jalom," Conférence internationale des African-istes de l'ouest, vol. V (1950), pp. 53-70.

"Traités conclus entre le Gouvernement française et des chefs des Rivières du Sud de 1884 à 1885," R. A. (1962), pp. 23-37.

Vignes, K. "Etude sur la rivalité d'influence entre les puissance européenes en Afrique équatoriale et occi-dentale depuis l'acte générale de Berlin jusqu'au seuil du XX$^e$ siècle," Revue française d'histoire d'outre-mer, vol. 48 (1961), pp. 5-95.

"Voyage au pays des Bagas et du Rio Nunez," Le Tour du monde, LI, 1$^{er}$ sem. (1886), pp. 273-304.

"Le Vrai Visage de Sanderval," R. A. , vol. 3 (1960), pp. 3-14.

Wallerstein, Immanuel M. "How Seven States Were Born in Former French West Africa," Africa Report, VI, no. 3 (March, 1961), pp. 3, 4, 7, 12, 15.

Weeks, George. "The Armies of Africa," Africa Report, IV (January, 1964), p. 11.

## GOVERNMENT DOCUMENTS

Dequecker, M. , La Guinée de la loi-cadre à l'indépendence. Paris: Centre Militaire d'Information et de Spécial-isation pour l'Outre-mer, 1960. Mech. dup.

DISSERTATIONS

Camara, L. P. "Les Structures de l'administration de la Guinée sous la colonisation française (1890-1958), Etude analytique et critique," Mémoire de fin d'études supérieures (Institut Polytechnique Gamal Abdel Nasser de Conakry (Ecole Supérieure d'Administration), 1967-68).

DuBois, Victor D. "The Independence Movement in Guinea; a study in African nationalism." Ph. D. Dissertation, Princeton University, 1962.

Kéita, S. K. "L'Etat de domination française en Guinée de 1945 à 1968," Cours de l'Institut polytechnique Gamal Abdel Nassar (Conakry), October, 1970. Mech dup.

## 4 ANTHROPOLOGY, ETHNOLOGY AND SOCIOLOGY

BOOKS

Attwood, William. The Reds and the Blacks. New York: Harper and Row, 1967.

Barbé, Raymond. Les Classes sociales en Afrique noire. Paris: Editions Sociales, 1964.

Baumann, Hermann, and Westermann, Diedrich. Les Peuples et les civilisations de l'Afrique. Paris: Payot, 1957.

Binet, Jacques. Les Soussous de Guinée. Paris: O. R. S. T. O. M. , 1960. ms.

Brasseur, G. , and Savonnet, G. Cartes ethno-démographiques de l'Afrique occidentale, feuille 2. Dakar: I. F. A. N. , 1960.

Bunot, Raoul Forêts du sud, Brindilles de la forêt toma. Mayenne: Collet, 1950.

Comité d'Etudes Historiques et Scientifiques de l'Afrique Occidentale Française. Coutumiers juridiques de l'Afrique occidentale française III: Mauritanie, Niger,

Côte d'Ivoire, Dahomey, Guinée française, Serie A.
Paris: Larose, 1939.

Condé, I. Groupements et rapports sociaux dous au comité
de Haute-Guinée: Komonida. Conakry: I. P. C. , 1966.

Decker, Henry de. Nation et développement communautaire
en Guinée et au Sénégal. Paris: Mouton, 1967.

Delafosse, Maurice. Enquête coloniale dous l'Afrique française occidentale et equatoriale sur l'organisation de
la famille indigène. Paris: 1930.

Derman, William. Serfs, Peasants and Socialists: A Former Serf Village in the Republic of Guinea. Berkeley:
University of California Press, 1973.

Dupire, Marguerite. Organisation sociale des Peul. Paris:
Plon, 1970.

Fréchou, Hubert. Le Régime foncier dans les Timbis et
dans la région du Moyen-Konkouré. Paris: O. R. S.
T. O. M. , 1961. M. S.

Froelich, Jean Claude. Animismes. Paris: Orante, 1964.

Gaisseau, P. Forêt sacrée; magie et rites secrets des To-
mas (Guinée française). Paris: Albin-Michel, 1953.

Guillabert, Lieutenant. Les Religions en Haute-Guinée. Doc-
ument from Centre de Hautes Etudes Administratives
sur l'Afrique et l'Asie Modernes. Paris: 1951. ms.

Hachten, William A. Muffled Drums: The News Media in
Africa. Ames: Iowa State University Press, 1971.

Hanry, Pierre. Erotisme Africain, I. Paris: Payot, 1970.

Hodge, Carleton T. (ed. ). Papers on the Manding. Bloomington: Indiana University, 1971.

Holas, Bohumil. Le Culte de Zié. Eléments de la religion
Kono. Dakar: I. F. A. N. , 1954.

_____. Les Masques Kono (Haute-Guinée française).
Paris: Geuthner, 1952.

Labouret, H.  Les Manding et leur langue.  Paris:  Larose, 1934.

Lee, J. M.  African Armies and Civil Order.  New York: Praeger, 1969.

Lelong, M. H.  Ces Hommes qu'on appelle anthropophages. Paris:  Alsatia, 1946.

Leroi-Gourhan, André, and Poirer, Jean.  Ethnologie de l'Union Française (Territoires Extérieurs) I:  Afrique. Paris:  P. U. F. , 1953.

Lestrange, Monique de.  Les Coniagui et les Bassari.  Paris:  P. U. F. , 1955.

Lévi-Strauss, Claude.  Le Totémisme aujourd'hui.  Paris: P. U. F. , 1962.

Mauny, Raymond.  Glossaire des expressions et termes locaux employés dous l'Ouest africain.  Dakar:  I. F. A. N. , 1954.

Moreira, José Mendes.  Fulas do Gabu, Memorias no. 6. Bissau:  Centro de estudos da Guiné portuguesa, 1948.

Morrison, Donald G. , et al.  Black Africa:  A Comparative Handbook.  New York:  Free Press, 1972.

Murdock, G. P.  Africa:  Its Peoples and Their Cultural History.  New York:  McGraw-Hill, 1959.

N'Diaye, Bokar.  Groupes ethniques au Mali.  Bamako:  Editions Populaires, 1970.

Niane, Djibril Tamsir.  Expédition archéologique à Niani. Conakry:  I. N. R. D. G. , 1965.  ms.

Ottenberg, Simon, and Ottenberg, Phoebe.  Cultures and Societies of Africa.  New York:  Random House, 1960.

Paulme, Denise.  Femmes d'Afrique noire.  Paris:  Mouton, 1960.

_____.  Les Gens du riz.  Paris:  Plon, 1954.

Rencontres internationales de Bouaké.  Tradition et modernisme en Afrique noire.   Paris:   Seuil, 1965.

Richard-Molard, J.   Problèmes humains en Afrique occi-
    dentale.   Paris:   P. A. , 1946.

Rivière, Claude.   Ethno-sociologie de la Basse-Guinée.   Con-
    akry:   I. P. C. , 1968.   Mech. dup.

_____.   Mutations sociales en Guinée.   Paris:   Rivière,
    1971.

Savineau, M.   Rapport sur la condition sociale de la femme
    indigène en Guinée française.   Dakar:   I. F. A. N. ,
    1938.   ms.

Les Sorciers-panthères.   Conakry:   Archives de l'I. N. R. D.
    G. , n. d. , MS.

Tagliaferri, Aldo, and Hammacher, Arno.   Fabulous Ances-
    tors:   Stone Carvings from Sierra Leone and Guinea.
    New York:   Africana Publishing, 1974.

Tauxier, Louis.   Moeurs et histoire des Peuls.   Paris:
    Payot, 1937.

Vieillard, Gilbert.   Notes sur les coutumes des Peuls au
    Fouta-Djalon.   Paris:   Larose, 1939.

Zolberg, Aristide R.   Creating Political Order; The Party-
    States of West Africa.   Chicago:   Rand McNally, 1966.


ARTICLES

André-Marie, Frère.   "De quelques coutumes barbares chez
    les Kissiens, "   La voix de Notre-Dame (October, 1926).

Appia, B.   "Les Forgerons du Fouta-Djalon, "   J. S. A. , XXXV
    (1965), pp. 317-352.

_____.   "Masques de Guinée française et de Casamance, "
    Journal Ouest Africain, 13 (1943), pp. 155-182.

Autra, M. T. R. and Sampil, M.   "Notes ethnographiques re-
    cueillies en pays kissien, "   R. A. , 3 (1960), pp. 58-67;
    1 (1961), pp. 50-58.

Balandier, G.  "Ethnologie et psychologie, "  E. G. , 1 (1947),
    pp. 47-54.

Balanghien, Etienne.  "Voie des ancêtres chez les Malinké"
    Vivant Univers, No. 267 (1970), pp. 22-31.

Balde, Chaikhou.  "Les Associations d'âge chez les Foulbé
    du Fouta-Djalon, "  Bull. I. F. A. N. , no. 1 (1939),
    pp. 89-109.

_____, Camara, Nene-Khaly, and Suret-Canale, J.  "Les
    Sites archéologiques de Guêmé-Sangan et Pêté-Bon-
    ôdji, "  R. A. , no. 3 (1962), pp. 51-68.

Bernus, Edmond.  "Kobané, un village malinké du Haut-
    Niger, "  C. O. M. , no. 35 (1956), pp. 239-262.

Binet, Jacques.  "Budgets familiaux africains, "  Cahiers de
    l'I. S. E. A. , serie "Humanités, " t. V (November, 1962),
    pp. 62-83.

_____.  "Foires et marchés en pays soussou, "  C. E. A. ,
    III (1962), pp. 104-114.

_____.  "Groupes socio-professionnels en Guinée, "  Le
    Monde non chrétien, no. 74 (April-June, 1965),  pp.
    67-93.

_____.  "Marchés africains, "  Cahiers de l'I. S. E. A. ,
    serie "Humanités, " I (November, 1959), pp. 67-85.

Boubakar, D. T.  "Le Divorce chez les Peuls au Fouta-Djal-
    lon, "  R. J. P. U. F. , 11 (1957), pp. 333-355.

Boutillier, J. L.  "Les Rapports du système foncier Toucou-
    ler et de l'organisation sociale et économique tradi-
    tionnelle:  leur évolution actuelle, "  African Agrarian
    Systems (1963), pp. 116-136.

Brass, William.  "The Demography of French-Speaking Ter-
    ritories, "  The Demography of Tropical Africa (1968),
    pp. 342-439.

C. , J.  "l'Alcoolisme en Guinée française, "  Zaire, 8 (1954),
    p. 857.

Cantrelle, Pierre, and Dupire, Marguerite.  "L'Endogamie

des Peuls du Fouta-Djalon," Population, no. 3 (1964), pp. 529-558.

Charles, Bernard. "Cadres politiques et administratifs dans la construction nationale en Guinée," Revue de l'Institut de Sociologie, IV, No. 2-3 (1967), pp. 345-353.

Cheron, G. "La Circoncision et l'excision chez les Malinké," Journal de la Société des Africanistes, 3 (1933), pp. 297-303.

Clavier, J. L. "Coutumier Coniagui," Bull. I. F. A. N., XIX (1952), pp. 321-336.

Corre, A. "Les Peuples du Rio Nunez," Revue d'anthropologie (1881), pp. 42-73.

Cournanel, Alain. "Situation de la classe ouvrière en République de Guinée," Partisans, No. 61 (September-October, 1971), pp. 119-136.

Coutouly, F. De. "Les Populations de l'ancien cercle de Touba-Kadé," E. G., no. 8 (1952), pp. 40-48.

_____. "Toucouleurs et Dialonké de Dinguiray," Bulletin de la Société de Géographie commerciale de Paris (1913), pp. 588-597.

"Coutumier soussou," Coutumier de l'A. O. F. (1939), pp. 575-610.

Crespin, M. "La Question du Coniagui," Revue indigène, no. 4 (1906), pp. 88-93.

Davies, O. "The Distribution of Old Stone-Age Material in Guinea," Bull. I. F. A. N., 21 (1959), pp. 102-108.

Delacour, A. "La Propriété et ses modes de transmission chez les Coniagui et les Bassari," E. G., no. 2 (1947), pp. 53-56.

_____. "Société secrètes chez les Tenda," E. G., no. 2 (1947), pp. 37-52.

_____. "Les Tenda (Koniagui, Bassari, Badyaranké) de la Guinée française," Revue d'ethnographie et de sociologie (1912), pp. 287-299; 370-381; (1913), pp. 31-52; 105-153.

"Les Densités de population au Fouta-Djalon," P. A. , 15 (1953), pp. 95-106.

Diallo, Ousmane. "Evolution sociale chez les Peuls du Fouta-Djalon," R. A. , no. 4 (1961), pp. 73-94.

Dobert, Margarita. "Guinea, the Role of Women," Africa Report, XIV, No. 7 (October, 1920), pp. 26-28.

_____. "Who Invaded Guinea?" Africa Report, XVI, No. 3 (March, 1971), pp. 16-18.

Duffner. "Croyances et coutumes religieuses chez les Guerzé et les Manon de la Guinée française," Bull. C. E. H. S. , no. 4 (1934), pp. 525-563.

"En Guinée française: le grenier de Conakry," Zaire, 6 (1952), pp. 975-976.

"Essai sur la vie paysanne au Fouta-Djalon," P. A. , 15 (1953), pp. 155-251.

Filipowiak, W. "L'Expédition archéologique polono-guinéenne à Niani," Africana Bulletin, 4 (1966), pp. 116-130.

Fode, P. "Le Révolution pacifique en marche: la nouvelle législation sociale de la République de Guinée," R. A. , 3 (1961), pp. 38-59.

Fodeba, K. "Chansons du Dioliba," P. A. , 4 (1948), pp. 595-598.

Foucault, Bertrand F. de. "Vers un réaménagement des relations entre les riverains du fleuve Sénégal," Revue de Défense Nationale, XXVIII, No. 2 (February, 1972), pp. 244-257.

Fréchou, Hubert. "Le régime foncier chez les Soussous du Moyen-Konkouré," Cahiers de l'I. S. E. A. , série "Humanités," no. 4 (1962), pp. 109-198.

_____. "Le Régime foncier des Timbis (Fouta-Djalon)," Etudes de droit africain et malgache. Etudes malgaches, no. 16 (1965), pp. 407-502.

Gamory-Dubourdeau, P. M. "Notice sur les coutumes des Toma," Bull. C. E. H. S. , no. 2 (1926), pp. 288-350.

Gavinet, M.  "Quelques Superstitions chez les Soussou de Basse-Guinée, " E. G. , 2 (1947), p. 67.

Germain, J.  "L'Au-Delà chez les Georzé, " E. G. , 2 (1947), pp. 27-35.

_____ .  "Extrait d'une monographie des habitants du Cercle de N'Zérékoré (Guerzé, Kono, Manon), " E. G. No. 13 (1955), pp. 3-54.

Gessain, Monique.  "Apropos de l'évolution actuelle des femmes Coniagui et Bassari, " J. S. A. , XXXIV, No. 11 (1964), pp. 258-276.

_____ .  "Etude socio-démographique du mariage chez les Coniagui et Bassari, " Bull. et Mem. Soc. anthropologie, V, XIᵉ serie (1963), pp. 5-85.

_____ .  "Note sur les Badiaranké, " J. S. A. , XXVIII, I-II (1963), pp. 43-89.

Gibbs, J. L.  "Poro Values and Courtroom Procedures in a Kpelle Chiefdom, " Sociologus, 18 (1962), pp. 341-350.

Guebhard, P.  "Les Peuls du Fouta-Djalon, " Revue d'étude ethnographique et sociologique, Vol. 2, 16-18 (April-June, 1909), pp. 85-105.

Guery, André.  "Les Classes sociales en Guinée, " Remarques Africaines, XXI, No. 365 (November 5, 1970), pp. 390-397.

"Guinée:  aujourd'hui, la revolution culturelle, " Jeune Afrique, No. 405 (October 7, 1968), pp. 37-38.

Holas, B.  "Danses masquées de la Basse-Côte, " E. G. , 1 (1947), pp. 61-67.

_____ .  "Décès d'une femme Guerzé (cercle de Nzérékoré, Guinée française), " Africa, 23 (1953), pp. 145-155; English summary, pp. 154-155.

_____ .  "Denkongo, dieu de la foudre des Kissiens, " Notes africaines, No. 36, n. d. , p. 12.

_____ .  "Echantillons du folklore Kono (Haute-Guinée

française), " E. G. 9 (1952), pp. 3-90.

_____. "Note complémentaire sur l'abri sous roche Blan-
dé (fouilles de 1951), " Bull. I. F. A. N. , 14 (1952),
pp. 1341-1352.

_____. "Notes préliminaires sur les fouilles de la grotte
de Blandé, " Bull. I. F. A. N. , 12 (1950), pp. 999-1006.

_____. "Pratiques divinatoires Kissi (Guinée Française),
Bull. I. F. A. N. , 14 (1952), pp. 272-308.

_____. "Quelques remarques complémentaires autour de
la circoncision kissi, " E. G. , 13 (1955), pp. 60-67.

_____, and Mauny, R. "Nouvelles Fouilles à l'abri sous
roche de Blandé (Guinée), " Bull. I. F. A. N. , 15 (1953),
pp. 1605-1618.

Houis, Maurice. "Les Minorités ethniques de la Guinée
côtière, " E. G. , no. 4 (1950), pp. 25-48.

_____. "Que sont les Soso?" E. G. , VI (1950), pp. 77-79.

_____. "Toponymie et sociologie, " Bull. I. F. A. N. , 22
(1960), pp. 443-445.

I. F. A. N. "Autour d'un casse-tête africain, " Bull. I. F. A. N. ,
14 (1952), pp. 358-362.

Keita, Mamadou Madeira. "La Famille et le mariage chez
les Tyapi, " E. G. , no. 2 (1947), pp. 63-66.

_____. "Le Noir et le secret, " E. G. , 1 (1947), pp. 69-
78.

Kourouma, Koly. "Le Revenu annuel d'une famille guerzé, "
E. G. , 1 (1947), pp. 55-59.

Lambin, R. "Notes sur les cérémonies et les épreuves
rituelles d'émancipation et d'initiation chez les Kissiens, " Bull. I. F. A. N. , 8 (1946), pp. 64-70.

Lassort, R. R. , and Lelong, P. P. "Chez les Kpélé du Liberia et les Guerzé de la Guinée française, " E. G. ,
no. 8 (1952), pp. 9-20.

Leriche, A. "Anthroponymie toucouleur," Bull. I. F. A. N.,
18 (1956), pp. 169-188.

Lerouge, R. P. "Le Pays Coniagui," Les missions catholiques (May-June, 1918).

Lestrange, M. De. "Contes et légendes des Fulakunda du
Badyar avec une introduction et des notes sur leurs
croyances et coutumes," E. G. (1951), pp. 3-66.

_____. "Génies de l'eau et de la brousse en Guinée fran-
çais," E. G., 4 (1950), pp. 3-24.

_____. "La Population de la région de Youkounkoun en
Guinée française," E. G. 7 (1951), pp. 67-69.

_____. "Pour une méthode socio-démographique (Etude
du mariage chez les Coniagui et les Bassari)," J. S. A.,
21 (1951), pp. 97-109.

_____. "Les Sarankolé de Badyar (technique de teintur-
iers)," E. G., 6 (1950), pp. 17-27.

_____. "Sociétés secrètes, circoncision et excision en
Afrique noire," Le Concours Médical (November,
1953), pp. 3815-3818.

Letnev, Artem. "Problème de l'évolution des rapports familiaux en Afrique occidentale," Revue internationale
des sciences sociales, no. 1 (1964), pp. 434-445.

Lhote, H. "L'Extraordinaire aventure des Peuls," P. A.,
N. S. 22 (1958), pp. 48-57.

Lombard, Jacques. "Tribalisme et integration nationale en
Afrique Noire," Homme et Societé, No. 12 (April-
June, 1969), pp. 69-86.

Madeira-Keita, M. "Aperçu sommaire sur les raisons de
la polygamie chez les Malinké," E. G., 4 (1950),
pp. 49-55.

Meillassoux, Claude. "Essai d'interpretation du phénomène
économique dans les sociétés traditionnelles d'auto-
subsistance," C. E. A., I (1960), p. 4.

_____. "Histoire et institutions du bafo de Bamako

d'après la tradition des Niaré," C. E. A. , 4 (1963), pp. 186-207.

Mengrelis, Thanos. "Esquisse sur l'habitat Guerzé," Africa, XXXIII, No. 1 (January, 1963), pp. 45-53.

_____. "Fête de la sortie d'excision en pays guerzé," Notes africaines, 50 (1951), pp. 11-13.

_____. "Le Sens des masques dans l'initiation chez les Guerzé de la Guinée Française," Africa, 22 (1952), pp. 257-262.

_____. "La Sortie des jeunes filles excisées en pays Mano [n]," E. G. , 8 (1952), pp. 55-58.

Moety, M. "Notes sur les Mani (Guinée française)," Bull. I. F. A. N. , XIX-B, 1-2, (1957), pp. 302-307.

Neel, H. "Notes sur deux peuplades de la frontière libérienne, les Kissi et les Toma," L'Anthropologie, XXIV (1913), pp. 445-475.

Niane, Djibril Tamsir. "Mise en place des populations de la Haute-Guinée," R. A. , No. 2 (1960), pp. 40-53.

"Notes démographiques sur la région de Labé," P. A. , 15 (1953), pp. 83-94.

"Organization, Motivating Forces of Society Discussed," Révolution Africaine (October 22-28, 1971), pp. 28-34, 37-38.

Paroisse, G. "Notes sur les peuplades autochtones de la Guinée française (Rivières du Sud)," L'Anthropologie, VII (1896), pp. 428-442.

Paulme, Denise. "Des riziculteurs africains, les Baga," C. O. M. (1957), pp. 257-278.

_____. "Les Kissi--'gens du riz;" P. A. 6 (1949), pp. 226-248.

_____. "Un Mouvement féminin en pays kissi," Notes africaines, 46, (April, 1950), p. 55.

_____. "La Notion de sorcier chez les Baga," Bull.

I. F. A. N., XX-B, Nos. 1-2 (January-April, 1958), pp. 406-416.

_____. "L'Initiation des jeunes filles en pays kissi," Conferencia internacional dos Africanistas (1952).

_____. "La Société Kissi: son organisation politique," C. E. A., I, No. 1 (January, 1960), pp. 75-85.

_____. "Structures sociales en pays Baga," Bull. I. F. A. N., XVIII-B, Nos. 1-2 (January-April, 1956), pp. 98-116.

Person, Yves. "Les Kissi et leurs statuettes de pierre dans le cadre de l'histoire ouest-africaine," Bull. I. F. A. N., XXIII-B, 1-2 (1961), pp. 1-59.

_____. "Soixante Ans d'évolution en pays Kissi," C. E. A., I, 1 (1960), pp. 86-114.

Poreko, D. O. "Evolution sociale chez les Peuls du Fouta-Djallon," R. A., 4 (1961), pp. 73-94.

Portères, R. "La Monnaie de fer dans l'Ouest africain au XX^e siècle," J. A. T. B. A., VII, nos. 1, 2, 3 (1960).

_____. "Un Problème d'ethnobotanique: relations entre le riz flottant du Rio Nunez et l'origine médi-nigér-ienne des Baga de Guinée française," J. A. T. B. A., nos. 10-11 (October-November, 1955), pp. 538-543.

"Rapport de la Commission des Programmes," Horoya, No. 1893 (May 5, 1972), pp. 3-4.

Richard-Molard, Jacques. "A propos de deux contes sous-sous," Notes africaines, 112 (October 1966), pp. 129-130.

_____. "Découverte de la Guinée," R. A., no. 4 (1961), pp. 8-23.

_____. "Démographie et structure des sociétés négro-peul, parmi les hommes libres et les 'serfs' du Fouta-Djalon (région de Labé, Guinée française)," Revue de géographie humaine et d'ethnologie, no. 4 (October, 1948-October, 1949), pp. 45-51.

_____. "Essai sur la vie paysanne au Fouta-Djalon,"
Revue de géographie alpine, XXXII, 2 (1944), pp. 135-
240.

Rivière, Claude. "Dixinn-Port, enquête sur un quartier de
Conakry," Bull. I. F. A. N. , XIX, Nos. 1-2 (January-
April, 1967), pp. 425-452.

_____. "Dynamique des systèmes fonciers et inégalités
sociales: le cas Guinéen," Cahiers Internationaux de
Sociologie, No. 20 (1973), pp. 61-94.

_____. "Fétischisme et démystification: l'exemple Gui-
néen," Afrique Documents, Nos. 102 and 103 (1969),
pp. 131-168.

_____. "Guinée: la difficile émergence d'un artisanat
caste," C. E. A. , XI, No. 36 (1969), pp. 600-625.

_____. "Les Incidents sociologiques du développement,"
Développement et Civilisations, No. 30 (June, 1967),
pp. 55-69.

_____. "La Mobilisation politique de la jeunesse Guiné-
enne," R. F. E. P. A. , No. 42 (June, 1969), pp. 67-89.

_____. "Les Résultats d'un enseignement révolutionnaire
en Guinée," R. F. E. P. A. , No. 52 (April, 1970), pp.
35-36.

_____. "Les Travailleurs de Wassa-Wassa: enquête sur
l'Entreprise Nationale de Tabacs et Allumettes," Canadian Journal of African Studies, II, No. 1 (Spring,
1968), pp. 81-96.

Roberty, M. "Quelques Règles de droit coutumier malinké
en Haute-Guinée," Bull. C. E. H. S. , 1-2 (1930), pp.
212-223.

Rutz, Werner. "Etnographisch-geographische Beobachtungen
im Stammesbereich der Nalu," Petermann's Mitteilungen, CIII, no. 4 (1959), pp. 273-276.

Saïdou, Baldé. "La Femme foulah et l'évolution," L'Education africaine, 98 (1937), pp. 214-219.

Saint-Père. "Création du royaume du Fouta-Djalon," Bull.

C. E. H. S. (1929), pp. 484-555.

_____. "Petit Historique des Sossoe du Rio Pongo," Bull. C. E. H. S. (1930), pp. 26-47.

Sampii, M. "Une Société secrète en pays nalou: Le Simo," R. A. , 1 (1961), pp. 46-49.

Schaeffner, A. "Musiques rituelles Baga," Congress of the International Society of Anthropology and Ethnology, 6, no. ii (1960), pp. 123-125.

_____. "Les Rites de circoncision en pays Kissi (Haute Guinée française)," E. G. , 12 (1953), pp. 3-56.

Schnell, Roland. "La Fête rituelle des jeunes excisées en pays baga," Notes africaines, no. 43 (1949), pp. 84-86.

_____. "Vestiges archéologiques et agriculture ancienne dans le Nord du Fouta-Djalon," Bull. I. F. A. N. , XIX-B, 1-2 (1957), pp. 295-301.

Silva, A. A. Da. "Arte Nalú," Boletim cultural da Guiné portuguesa, 11, no. 44 (1956), pp. 27-47.

Stainer, M. "Notice sur les Coniagui," E. G. , 2 (1947), pp. 57-61.

Suret-Canale, J. "Les Fondements sociaux de la vie politique africaine contemporaine," Recherches internationales, no. 22, XI-XII (1960), pp. 6-56.

_____. "Les Noms de famille toma," R. A. (August-September, 1963), pp. 34-35.

Suzzoni, Jean. "Monographie de l'île de Kaback," La Guinée française (August 5-25, 1948).

Szumowski, G. "Fouilles de l'Abri sous roche de Kourouunkorokalé (Soudan français)," Bull. I. F. A. N. , 18 (1956), pp. 462-508.

Techer, H. "Coutumes des Tendas," Bull. C. E. H. S. , no. 4 (1933), pp. 630-666.

Telli, Diallo. "Le Divorce chez les Peuls," P. A. , n. s. (October-November 1958), pp. 29-47.

Teullière, G. "Alpha Yaya et la politique indigène," Revue indigène (1911), pp. 615-620.

Thomas, Louis-Vincent. "L'Africain et le sacré," Bull. I. F. A. N., XXIX-B, 3-4 (1967), pp. 620-623.

_____. "Philosophie de la religion négro-africaine traditionnelle," Afrique-Documents, 79 (1965).

"Les Traits d'ensemble du Fouta-Djalon," P. A., 15 (1953), pp. 141-154.

Verdat, M. "Le Ouali de Goumba," E. G., no. 3 (1949), pp. 3-81.

Vieillard, Gilbert. "Notes sur les Peuls du Fouta-Djalon," Bull. I. F. A. N., II (1940), pp. 87-210.

Wane, Y. "Etat actuel de la documentation au sujet des Toucouleurs," Bull. I. F. A. N., 25 (1963), pp. 457-477.


GOVERNMENT DOCUMENTS

Guinea. Ministère de la Santé et es Affaires Sociales. "Développement des services sanitaires et sociaux," Conakry: 1966. Mech. dup.

Yugoslavia. Institut d'Urbanisme. Plan d'urbanisme de Conakry, Lagreb: 1963.


DISSERTATIONS

Charles, Bernard. "Cadres guinéens et appartenances ethniques." Unpublished thèse de doctorat, 3e cycle, Sorbonne, 1968.

Diallo, Thierno. Les Institutions politiques du Fouta-Djalon. Unpublished thèse dectorat, 3e cycle, Sorbonne, 1968.

Dobert, Margarita. "Civic and Political Participation of Women in French Speaking West Africa." Unpublished doctoral dissertation, George Washington University, 1970.

Fofana, Mamadou Lamire. "Le Divorce en droit guinéen. "

Unpublished dissertation, L. P. C. , 1968.    Mech. dup.

## 5 CONTEMPORARY POLITICS

BOOKS

L'Agression portugaise contre la République de Guinée.    Con-
    akry:  I. N. R. D. G. , 1971.

Ainslie, Rosalynde.    The Press in Africa.    New York:   Wal-
    ker, 1967.

Ansprenger, Franz.    Politik in Schwarzen Afrika.    Cologne:
    Westdeutscher Verlag, 1961.

Bell, M. J. V.    Army and Nation in Sub-Saharan Africa.    (Adel-
    phi Papers, No. 21.)  London:  International Institute
    for Strategic Studies, August, 1965.

_____.  Military Assistance to Independent African States.
    (Adelphi Papers, No. 15.)  London:  International In-
    stitute for Strategic Studies, 1970.

Carter, Gwendolen M.  (ed.).    African One-Party States.
    Ithaca, N. Y. :   Cornell University Press, 1962.

Condé, Alpha.    Guinée:  Albanie d'Afrique ou néo-colonie
    américaine  Paris:   Editions Gît-ce Coeur, 1972.

Diakité, Claude A.    Guinée enchaînée ou le livre noir de
    Sékou Touré.   Paris:   Diané, 1972.

Diawara, A.  Guinée, la marche du peuple.    Dakar:   Ed-
    ition Cerda, 1968.

Du Bois, Victor D.    The Decline of the Guinean Revolution,
    Part I:  The Beginnings of Disillusionment.  (Ameri-
    can Universities Field Staff Reports, West Africa Ser-
    ies, VIII, No. 7.)  New York:  A. U. F. S. , November,
    1965.

_____.  The Decline of the Guinean Revolution, Part II:
    Economic Development and Political Expediency. (Am-
    erican Universities Field Staff Reports, West Africa
    Series, VIII, No. 8.)  New York: A. U. F. S. , Decem-
    ber, 1965.

. The Decline of the Guinean Revolution, Part III: The Erosion of Public Morality. (American Universities Field Staff Reports, West Africa Series, VIII) New York: A. U. F. S., December, 1965.

. The Problems of Independence: The Decolonization of Guinea. (American Universities Field Staff Reports, West Africa Series, Guinea, V, No. 8.) New York: A. U. F. S., 1962.

. The Rise of an Opposition to Sékou Touré, Part I: Reform and Repression by the Parti Démocratique de Guinée. (American Universities Field Staff Reports, West Africa Series, IX, No. 1.) New York: A. U. F. S., March, 1966.

. The Rise of an Opposition to Sékou Touré, Part II: The Estrangement Between the Leaders and the People of Guinea. (American Universities Field Staff Reports, West Africa Series, IX, No. 2.) New York: A. U. F. S., March, 1966.

. The Rise of an Opposition to Sékou Touré, Part III: The Plot Against the Government and the Accusations Against the Council of the Entente and France. (American Universities Field Staff Reports, West Africa Series, IX, No. 3.) New York: A. U. F. S., March, 1966.

. The Rise of an Opposition to Sékou Touré, Part IV: The Entente's Reactions to the Guinean Accusations. (American Universities Field Staff Reports, West Africa Series, IX, No. 4.) New York: A. U. F. S., April, 1966.

. The Rise of an Opposition to Sékou Touré, Part V: The Formation of a Common Front Against Guinea by the Ivory Coast and Ghana. (American Universities Field Staff Reports, West Africa Series, IX, No. 5.) New York: A. U. F. S., April, 1966.

. The Rise of an Opposition to Sékou Touré, Part VI: The Activation of the Guinean Exiles: The Front de Libération Nationale de Guinée (F. L. N. G.). (American Universities Field Staff Reports, West Africa Series, IX, No. 7.). New York: A. U. F. S., July, 1966.

_____. Thaw in the Tropics: France and Guinea Move Toward a Rapprochement. (American Universities Field Staff Reports, West Africa Series, Guinea, VI, No. 2.) New York: A. U. F. S. , 1963.

Egyptian Society of International Law. Constitutions of the New African States. Cairo: The Society, 1962.

Gavrilov, N. La République de Guinée. Moscow: Editions de Littérature Orientale, 1961.

Gigon, Fernand. Guinée; Etat pilote. Paris: Plon, 1959.

Hodgkin, Thomas. African Political Parties. London: Penguin, 1961.

International Institute for Strategic Studies. The Military Balance 1973-74. London: The Institute, 1974.

Jalloh, A. A. Political Integration in French-Speaking Africa. Berkeley: Institute of International Studies, University of California, 1973.

Krueger, Heinz, and Umann, Joachim. Blende auf für Guinea. Leipzig: F. A. Brockhaus Verlag, 1961.

Legvold, Robert. Soviet Policy in West Africa. Cambridge, Mass. : Harvard University Press, 1970.

Liebermann, Henri. La République de Guinée, une expérience d'émancipation africaine. Antwerp: I. S. C. E. A. , 1961. Mech. dup.

Lusignan, Guy. French-Speaking Africa Since Independence. New York: Praeger, 1969.

Mabileau, A. , and Meyriat, I. (eds. ). Décolonisation et régimes politiques en Afrique noire. Paris: Foundation des Nationale Sciences Politiques, 1967.

Morgenthau, Ruth Schachter. Political Parties in French-Speaking West Africa. Oxford, England: Oxford University Press, 1964.

Parti Démocratique de Guinée. Status du P. D. G. Conakry: P. D. G. , 1969.

Peter, J.   Annuaire des états d'Afrique noire--gouvernment
et cabinets ministériels des républiques d'expression
française.   Paris:   Ediafric, 1961.

Salacuse, Jeswald W.   An Introduction to Law in French-
Speaking Africa, I:   French-Speaking Africa South of
the Sahara.   Charlottesville, Va.:  Michie, 1969.

Segal, Ronald.   Political Africa:  A Who's Who of Personal-
ities and Parties.   New York:  Praeger, 1961.

Skogan, Wesley.   Bibliography on Party Politics in Guinea,
1950-1962.   Evanston, Ill.:  Northwestern University,
International Comparative Political Parties Project,
1967.

Sy, S.   Recherches sur l'exercice du pouvoir politique en
Afrique-Côte d'Ivoire, Guinée, Mali.   Paris:   Editions A. Pedonne, 1964.

Tanine, S.   L'Edification de l'Etat de la République de Guinée.   Moscow:   Editions d'Etat de Littérature Juridique, 1960.   (In Russian.)

Thomas, L. V.   Le Socialisme et l'Afrique.   Paris:   Le Livre africain, 1966.

Touré, Ahmed Sékou.   L'Action politique du Parti démocratique de Guinée, 18 vols.   Conakry:  I. N. R. D. G.,
1958-1972.

_____.   II$^e$ Congrès national de la J. R. D. A.   (Conakry,
les 14, 15 et 16 sept. 1961).   Conakry:  Impr. nat.,
1961.

_____.   Discours commémoratif de la proclamation de la
République de Guinée (II$^e$ anniversaire de l'indépendance nationale), 2 oct. 1961.   Conakry:  Impr. nat.,
1961.

_____.   Discours d'ouverture, III$^e$ Conférence mondiale
des enseignants, 27 juill. 1960.   Conakry:  Impr.
nat., 1960.

_____.   8 novembre 1964.   Conakry:  Impr. nat. Patrice-
Lumumba, 1964.

_____. La Lutte du Parti démocratique de Guinée pour l'émancipation africaine, Vol. VI. Conakry: Impr. nat., 1961.

_____. Poèmes militants. Conakry: Impr. nat. Patrice-Lumumba, 1964.

_____. Le Pouvoir populaire, Vol. XVI. Conakry: Impr. nat. Patrice-Lumumba, 1968.

_____. Rapport de doctrine et de politique générale (V^e Congrès national du P. D. G. -R. D. A. tenu à Conakry les 14, 15, 16, et 17 sept. 1959). Conakry: Impr. nat., 1958.

_____. Rapport de doctrine et d'orientation (Conférence nationale de Conakry des 14, 15, 16 et 17 août 1961). Conakry: Impr. nat., 1961.

_____. Rapport d'orientation et de doctrine présenté au Congrès général de l'U. F. T. A. N., tenu à Conakry du 15 au 18 janvier 1959. Conakry: Impr. nat., 1959.

_____. La Technique de la Révolution, Vol. XVIII. Conakry: Impr. nat. Patrice-Lumumba, 1972.

_____. Texte des interviews accordés aux représentants de la presse. Conakry: Impr. nat., 1959.

United Nations. Foreign Trade Statistics of Africa. Series A. Direction of Trade. New York: Economic Commission for Africa, 1962.

Voss, Joachim. Der Progressistische Entwicklungstaat: Das Beispiel der Republik Guinea (Vol. 81 of the papers of the Friedrich Ebert Foundation.) Hanover: Verlag für Literature und Zeitgeschehen, 1971.

ARTICLES

"Action conjointe dans le Fouta-Djalon (Mamou, République de Guinée, 2-7 mai 1960)," R. A., 3 (1960), pp. 15-57.

Adamolekun, 'Lapido. "Politics and Administration in West Africa: The Guinean Model," Journal of Administration Overseas, VIII, No. 4 (October, 1969), pp. 235-242.

_____ . "Some Reflections on Sékou Touré's Guinea, "
West Africa (March 19 and 26, April 2 and 9, 1973).

Adrian, Charles F.  "Political Thought of Sékou Touré, "
African Political Thought (1968), pp. 101-135.

Africa Research Bulletin.  London (monthly).

African Development.  London (monthly).

"Agence guinéenne de presse, " Guinée actualités (1967--ir-
regular).

"Air Forces of the World, Part 5:  North and West Africa, "
Interavia, XXIV, No. 1 (January, 1974), pp. 71-74.

"Airmen Going to USSR for Training Courses, " Journal Officiel de la République de Guinée (February 15, 1972),
pp. 26-27.

Ameillon, B.  "Vérités sur la Guinée ou contre-vérités sur
la décolonisation, " Partisans, no. 19 (February-March,
1965), pp. 37-43.

Andrain, C.  "Guinea and Senegal:  contrasting types of African socialism, " African Socialism (1964), pp. 160-
174.

Beaujeu-Garnier, J.  "Essai de géographie électorale guinéenne, " C. O. M. , no. 44 (1958), pp. 309-333.

_____ . "Guinée indépendante, " Revue politique et parle-
mentaire, no. 684 (November, 1958), pp. 353-361.

Benot, Y.  "L'Afrique en mouvement: la Guinée à l'heure de
plan" La Pensée, No. 94 (November-December, 1960),
pp. 3-36

Berg, Eliot J.  "The Economic Basis of Political Choice in
French West Africa, " American Political Science Review, LIV, 2 (June, 1960), pp. 391-405.

_____ . "The Political Thought of Sékou Touré, " African
Political Thought:  Lumumba, Nkruma, and Touré
(1968), pp. 101-147.

_____ . "Socialism and Economic Development in Tropical

Africa," Quarterly Journal of Economics, LXXVIII (1964), pp. 549-573.

Bornstein, R. "Organization of Senegal River States," Journal of Modern African Studies, X, No. 2 (July, 1972), pp. 267-283.

Buchmaus, Jean. "Régimes politiques d'Afrique noire," Zaire, Revue Congolaise (1960), pp. 283-306.

"Causes, Effects of Guineans' Exodus Discussed," Remarques Africaines (November 25, 1971).

Césaire, Aimé. "La Pensée politique de Sékou Touré," P. A., XXIX (December, 1959-January, 1960), pp. 65-74.

Charles, Bernard. "Cadres politiques et administratifs dans la construction nationale en Guinée," Revue de l'Institut de Sociologie, IV, Nos. 2-3 (1967), pp. 345-353.

_____. "Un Parti politique africain: Le Parti démocratique de Guinée," Revue française des sciences politiques, XII, No. 2 (June, 1962).

"Communique Describes 2d Session of PDG Central Committee," Horoya (May 27, 1972), pp. 2, 4.

Cournanel, Alain. "Situation de la classe ouvrière en République de Guinée," Partisans, No. 61 (September-October, 1971), pp. 119-136.

Craene, Philippe de. "'Le Dialogue avec Conakry se poursuit' déclare Président Houphouet-Boigny," Le Monde (July 28, 1972), p. 1.

"Decree Establishes Police Services Bureau," Journal Officiel de la République de Guinée (July 1, 1974), p. 161.

Diallo, Alpha Abdoulaye. "Introduction à l'étude de la Constitution guinéenne," R. A., no. 2 (1960), pp. 52-58.

Dubois, Jacques. "Guinée, An I," Horizons, vol. 9, no. 104 (January, 1960), pp. 58-67.

Du Bois, Victor D. "The Role of the Army in Guinea,"

Africa Report, VIII, No. 1 (January, 1963), pp. 3-5.

"Eighth District Officials Purged," Horoya (August 31-September 7, 1974), pp. 38-39.

Europe-Outremer. Paris (monthly).

"La Femme guinéenne, militante du P. D. G. ," Cahier du militant, 21, n. d. , p. 13.

Fischer, Georges. "Quelques Aspects de la doctrine politique guinéenne," Civilisations, Vol. IX, no. 4 (1959), pp. 457-478.

_____. "La Signification de l'independance guinéenne," P. A. , XXIX (December, 1959-January, 1960), pp. 53-61.

François, Claire. "L'Indépendance de la Guinée," Cahiers internationaux, no. 100 (November, 1958), pp. 1-14.

Gastaud, Maurice. "Naissance et évolution du Parti démocratique de Guinée," Cahiers du Centre d'études et de recherches marxistes, no. 55, n. d.

"Guinée, prélude à l'indépendance," P. A. (1958).

Hamon, Léo. "Le Parti démocratique de Guinée, d'avant l'indépendance à 1960," Revue juridique et politique d'outre-mer, 15, no. 3 (1961), pp. 354-368.

Hodgkin, Thomas, and Schachter, Ruth. "French-Speaking West Africa in Transition," International Conciliation, no. 528 (May, 1960), pp. 375-436.

Industries et Travaux d'Outre-Mer. Paris (monthly),

Johnson, R. W. "The PDG and the Mamou Deviation," African Perspectives (1970), pp. 347-369.

_____. "Sékou Touré and the Guinean Revolution," African Affairs, 69 (October, 1970), pp. 350-365.

Journal officiel de la Guinée française. Conakry (weekly 1899-1958).

Journal officiel de la République de Guinée. Conakry (fortnightly, 1958-).

Julit, A.   "Conférence sur la Guinée, bilan d'une indépen-
    dance," Partisans, no. 19 (February-March, 1965),
    pp. 33-37.

"Justice in Guinea," Review of the International Commission
    of Jurists, No. 7 (December, 1971), pp. 4-8.

Kaba, Lansiné.   "Guinean Politics:  A Critical Historical
    Overview," Journal of Modern African Studies, vol.
    15, no. 1 (March 1977).

"Kissidougou Federal Bureau Purged and Reorganized," Hor-
    oya (June 13, 1974), pp. 1-2.

Marcum, John A.   "Report from Guinea," New Leader, XLI,
    No. 44 (December 1, 1958), pp. 3-7.

Miandre, J.   "L'Expérience guinéenne," Espirit, 10 (October,
    1963), pp. 514-531.

"Military Men to USSR," Journal Officiel de la République de
    Guinée (October 1, 1972), pp. 167-168.

"Military-Paramilitary Committees' Duties Defined," Horoya
    (August 10-17, 1974), pp. 43-44.

Le Mois en Afrique:  Revue Française d'Etudes Politiques
    Africaines.  Dakar and Paris (monthly).

Perroux, François.   "Une Nation en voie de se faire:  la
    République de Guinée," Revue de l'action populaire,
    no. 129 (June, 1959), pp. 683-705.

"President Describes Army's Social and Economic Role,"
    Horoya (February 19, 1974), pp. 1-2.

President Touré Reviews Information Organs, Suggests Im-
    provements," Horoya-Hebdo (February 26-March 3,
    1972), pp. 3-27.

"Les P.R.L.," Horoya-Hebdo (July 13-20, 1974), pp. 34-41.

Quarterly Review of Labour Problems in Africa.  Brazza-
    ville (quarterly).

"Quelques Aspects du problème des cadres en Republique de
    Guinée," R.A., 4 (October-December, 1960), pp. 40-
    47.

Rabemananjara, J.  "Variations sur le thème guinéen,"
P. A. , 29 (1959-1960), pp. 75-88.

"Réorganisation de la Justice," Horoya (August 25, 1973),
pp. 4-7.

Rivière, Claude.  "Les Mécanismes de constitution d'une
bourgeoisie commerçante en République de Guinée,"
C. E. A. , XI, 43 (1971), pp. 378-399.

_____.  "La Politique étrangère de la Guinée," R. F. E.
P. A. , No. 68 (August, 1971), pp. 37-68.

_____.  "Purges et complots au sein du PDG," R. F. E.
P. A. , No. 95 (November, 1973), pp. 31-45.

_____.  "Théorie de la dynamique conflictuelle dans les
nouveaux etats.  Réflexions à propos du cas guinéen,"
Cultures et développement, II, 3-4 (1969-1970), pp.
657-678.

Sainville, Léonard.  "La Presse française et la Guinée,"
P. A. , XXIX (December, 1959-January, 1960), pp.
109-116.

"Les Statuts du Parti Démocratique de Guinée," R. A. , 4
(1963), pp. 34-47.

Suret-Canale, Jean.  "L'Afrique à l'heure de l'indépendance
et la communauté rénovée," Cahiers du Communisme,
36e année, no. 11 (November, 1960), pp. 1735-1761.

_____.  "La Guinée face à son avenir," Nouvelle revue
internationale (Prague), no. 90 (June, 1966), pp. 58-
75.

_____.  "Les Relations internationales de la République
de Guinée," Foreign Relations of African States (1974),
pp. 259-276.

_____.  "République de Guinée, un an d'indépendance,"
La Nouvelle Critique, no. 109 (September-October,
1959), pp. 33-67.

_____.  "Vérités sur la Guinée," Cahiers du communisme
(réponse à B. Ameillon) (October, 1964), pp. 56-67.

Touré, S.  "The Republic of Guinea, " International Affairs,
    36 (1960), pp. 168-173.

"Touré Discusses Militia Organization, " Horoya (March 31,
    1974), pp. 3-4.

Vernay, A.  "La Guinée dans le sillage de Sékou Touré, "
    Les Echos (July 10, 1961).

"Vers la normalisation des rapports Franco-Guinéens, "
    Marchés Tropicaux et Méditerrannéens (January 31,
    1975), pp. 249-250.

"Violemment mis en cause par M. Sékou Touré:  Sénégal et
    Côte d'Ivoire, "  Le Monde (September 20, 1973), pp.
    1-8

Wallerstein, I.  "The Political Ideology of the PDG, " P. A. ,
    XL, 1 (1962), pp. 30-41.

West Africa.  London (weekly).

Whiteman, Kaye.  "Guinea in West African Politics, " The
    World Today, XXVII, No. 8 (August, 1971), pp. 350-
    358.

World Agricultural Economics and Rural Sociology Abstracts.
    Oxford, England (monthly).


GOVERNMENT DOCUMENTS

Guinea.  La Guinée Nouvelle, Conakry (irregular).

_____.  Statut du PDG, Edition 1969 Permanence nationale.
    Conakry:  Imprimerie Nationale Patrice Lumumba, 1969.

_____.  Statut particulier des divers cadres uniques, Con-
    akry:  Imprimerie Nationale Patrice Lumumba, n. d.

_____.  Textes des interviews accordées par le Prési-
    dent Sékou Touré, Conakry:  April, 1959.  Mech. dup.

_____.  Ministère de la Fonction Publique et du Travail.
    Etat des fontionaires guinéens en service avant l'in-
    dépendance, Conakry:  August, 1964.  Mech. dup.

_____. Ministère de l'Intérieur [Territoire de la Guinée.] Nouvelle Structure Administrative, Conakry: Imprimerie du Gouvernment, 1958.

_____. _____. La Vérité sur les évênements de la Guinée, Conakry: 6 mai 1958. Mech. dup.

_____. Parti Démocratique de Guinée-RDA. Bulletin d'information du BPN (formerly Bulletin du compterendu des activités du BPN), Conakry (irregular, 1962- ).

_____. _____. Huitième congrès du Parti démocratique de Guinée (RDA), tenu à Conakry du 25 septembre au 20 octobre 1967, Conakry: Imprimerie Nationale Patrice Lumumba, n. d.

United States. Agreement between the United States of America and Guinea effected by exchange of notes signed at Washington, October 28, 1959, U. S. Gov. Printing Office, 1959.


DISSERTATIONS

Adamolekun, O. O. "Central Government Administration in Guinea and Senegal Since Independence: A Comparative Study." D. Phil. Thesis, University of Oxford, 1972.

Bah, T. O. "Etude du système du budgets locaux et d'arrondissements appliqué aux régions administratives de Conakry et Forécariah." Unpublished dissertation, I. P. C. (E. S. A.), 1969-70.

Charles, B. "Cadres guinéens et appartenance ethnique." Unpublished Ph. D. dissertation, Fondation Nationale des Science Politique, 1968.

Diallo, A. L. "L'Evolution des institutions administrative de la République de Guinée de 1958 à 1968." Unpublished dissertation, I. P. C. (E. S. A.), 1967-68.

Dioubaté, M. L. "Les Institutions politiques de la République de Guinée." Unpublished dissertation, I. P. C. (E. S. A.), 1966-67.

Douno, M.   "Le Rapport du parti avec i'Etat guinéen. "   Unpublished dissertation, I. P. C. (E. S. A. ), 1969-70.

Kourouma, K. R.   "L'Evolution des institutions judiciares en
Guinée. "   Unpublished dissertation, I. P. C.  (E. S. A. ),
1967-68.


## 6 ECONOMICS


## BOOKS

Amin, Samir.   Le Mali, La Guinée et le Ghana:  trois expériences africaines de développement.   Paris:  P. U.
F. , 1965.

Banque Internationale pour la Reconstruction et le Développement.  The Economy of Guinea.  Washington:  B. I. R.
D. , 1966.  Mech. dup.

Bettelheim, Charles.   Directives générales à suivre par les
régions et les villages dans l'élaboration du plan tri-
ennal guinéen.   Conakry:  I. N. R. D. G. , 1959.  Mech.
dup.

Bureau de Développement pour la Production Agricole.   Textes relatifs au développement rural.   Paris:  Caisse
Centrale de Coopération Economique, 1962.  Mech.
dup.

De Decker, H.   Nation et développement en Guinée et au
Sénégal.   The Hague:  Mouton, 1967.

La Dépêche Coloniale.   Comment se pose le problème agricole en A. O. F. et plus particulièrement en Guinée.
Paris:  1924.

Dumont, René.   Afrique noire:  développement agricole:  ré-
conversion de l'économie agricole:  Guinée, Côte d'Ivoire, Mali.   Paris:  P. U. F. , 1962.

_____ .   Etude provisoire des actions d'urgence agricoles
en quelques points de Guinée.   1959.  Mech. dup.

Fabre, M.   Note sur l'industrialisation de la Guinée française.   1956.  Mech. dup.

Firsov, A. A.  Les Problèmes économiques de la République
    de Guinée.  Moscow:  Editions "Science, " 1965.  (In
    Russian. )

Goldman, Marshall I.  Soviet Foreign Aid.  New York:  Prae-
    ger, 1967.

Harbison, Frederick, and Myers, Charles A. (eds. ).  Man-
    power and Education:  Country Studies in Economic
    Development.  New York:  McGraw-Hill, 1965.

Haut commissariat de l'A. O. F.  Etude sur les échanges rou-
    tiers en Guinée française.  Dakar:  Haut commissariat
    de l'A. O. F. , 1957.

I. F. A. N.  Etudes agricoles et économiques de quatre villages
    de Guinée française.  Dakar:  I. F. A. N. , 1956.

International Labor Office.  African Labor Survey (Studies
    and Reports, New Series, No. 48).  Geneva:  Inter-
    national Labor Organization, 1958.

Johnson, H. (ed. ).  Economic Nationalism in Old and New
    States.  Chicago:  University of Chicago Press, 1967.

Leynaud, Emile.  Contribution à l'étude des structures so-
    ciales et de la modernisation rurale dans la haute
    vallée du Niger.  Paris:  Bureau de Développement
    pour la Production Agricole, 1964, 3 vols.  Mech.
    dup.

Meynaud, J. , and Salah-Bey, A.  Le Syndicalisme africain.
    Paris:  Payot, 1963.

November, A.  L'Evolution du mouvement syndical en Af-
    rique occidentale.  Paris:  Mouton, 1965.

Organisation for Economic Cooperation and Development.
    Development Cooperation:  1972 Review; _____ ,
    1973 Review.  Paris:  O. E. C. D. , 1972, 1973.

_____ .  Geographical Distribution of Financial Flows to
    Less-Developed Countries.  Paris;  O. E. C. D. , 1965.

Quarterly Economic Review:  Senegal, Mali, Mauritania, and
    Guinea, Nos. 2, 3, and 4.  London:  The Economist,
    December, 1974.

Reconversion de l'économie agricole: Guinée, Côte-d'Ivoire, Mali. Paris: P. U. F., 1961.

Stokke, Baard Richard. Soviet and Eastern European Trade and Aid in Africa. New York: Praeger, 1967.

Touré, Ismaël. Le Développement économique de la République de Guinée. Conakry: I. N. R. D. G., 1964. Mech. dup.

United Nations. Economic Commission for Africa. Summaries of Economic Data, Fifth Year, No. 14 (Guinea). Addis Ababa: Economic Commission for Africa, December, 1973.

Villiaume, M. Etude des gîtes aurifères de la Guinée française, 1905-1906. Paris: Imprimerie de la Banque et des Compagnies d'Assurances, 1908.

Yansane, Hamy Mouké Layah. L'Industrialisation de la République de Guinée. Paris: 1962. ms.


## ARTICLES

Africa: An International Business, Economic and Political Monthly. London (monthly).

Alpha, D. "Perspectives sur l'élevage en République de Guinée," R. A., 1-4 (1959), pp. 47-62.

Amin, Samir. "Guinea: Economy," Africa South of the Sahara, 1973 (1973), pp. 397-404.

Badouin, R. "A la recherche d'un système économique en Guinée," Droit social (January, 1963), pp. 11-21.

Balandier, G. "L'Or de la Guinée française," P. A., 4 (1948), pp. 539-548.

Balde, S. "L'Elevage au Fouta-Djallon (régions de Timbo et Labé)," Bull. I. F. A. N., 1 (1939), pp. 630-644.

Barthe, M. "Le Labour attelé en Guinée française," Agronomie tropicale, nos. 1-2, (January-February, 1951), pp. 73-76.

"La Bauxite et le fer dans l'économie guinéenne," Industries et travaux d'outre-mer, no. 106 (September, 1961), pp. 701-705.

Beaujeu-Garnier, J. "L'agriculture guinéenne," L'Information géographique (November-December, 1958), pp. 185-198.

Benot, Yves. "La Guinée à l'heure du plan," La Pensée, no. 94 (November-December, 1960), pp. 3-36.

Berg, Eliot J. "French West Africa," Labor and Economic Development (1959), pp. 186-259.

Binet, J. "Marchés en pays Soussou," C. E. A. , 3 (1962), pp. 104-114.

Bodin, F. "Où en sont les projets industriels de Guinée?" Industries et travaux d'outre-mer, no. 66 (May, 1959), pp. 262-266.

C. , J. "Combinat industriel en Guinée française," Zaire, 8 (1954), p. 642.

Charles, Bernard. "La Guinée," Décolonisation et régimes politiques en Afrique noire (1967), pp. 159-204.

_____. "Un Parti politique africain, le parti démocratique de Guinée," Revue française de science politique, 12, 2 (June, 1962), pp. 312-359.

Charrière, Jacques. "Une Expérience de planification, la Guinée," Cahiers internationaux, no. 117 (March-April, 1961), pp. 65-88.

"Le Développement minier de l'Afrique francophone," Europe-France-outre-mer, no. 411 (April, 1964), pp. 9-54.

Diallo, Alpha. "Perspectives sur l'élevage en République de Guinée," R. A. (1959), pp. 47-62.

Direction of Trade. Washington (monthly).

Dresch, Jean. "La Riziculture en Afrique occidentale," A. G. (1949), pp. 295-312.

Edwards, John. "Bauxite Supplies Concern," Financial Times (September 24, 1974), p. 18.

"Entreprise minière en Guinée française," Zaire, 7 (1953), pp. 75-76.

Friedland, William H.  "Paradoxes of African Trade Union-ism," Africa Report (June, 1965), pp. 6-13.

Grisoni, A.  La Main-d'oeuvre guinéenne," Industries et travaux d'outre-mer, no. 46 (September, 1957), pp. 635-637.

Hauser, A.  "Les Industries extractives en Guinée," E. G., no. 13 (1955), pp. 55-59.

Hazard, John N.  "Guinea's Non-Capitalist Way," Columbia Journal of Transnational Law, V, No. 2 (1966), pp. 231-262.

Hirschfeld, André.  "Le Rôle du mouvement coopératif dans la commercialisation de la banane en République de Guinée," Revue des études coopératives, no. 143 (1966), pp. 33-44.

_____.  "Sur quelques expériences coopératives ou pré-coopératives en Afrique noire," Revue des études co-opératives, no. 139, 1er trim. (1965), pp. 39-60.

Hodgkinson, Edith.  "Guinea: Economy," Africa South of the Sahara, 1974 (1974), pp. 378-384.

"L'Industrie et les exportations...," Europe-France-outre-mer, no. 417 (October, 1964), pp. 15-18.

"Les Industries alimentaires en Guinée," Revue du développe-ment économique, no. 4 (November, 1964), pp. 17-20.

Kourouma, K.  "Le Revenu annuel d'une famille guerzé," E. G., 1 (1947), pp. 55-59.

Lamine, T. M.  "Les Ports de Guinée," R. A., 1-4 (1959), pp. 63-69.

Leduc, G.  "L'Application de la notion de "pôle de développe-ment" aux ensembles industriels de l'Afrique subsa-harienne," Marchés tropicaux, no. 615 (August 24, 1957), pp. 2029-2032.

Leunda, Xavier.  "La Réforme de l'enseignement et son in-

cidence sur l'évolution rurale en Guinée," <u>Civilisa-</u>
<u>tions,</u> XXII, No. 2 (1972), pp. 232-262.

Noumouke, D.  "Le Service de l'élevage et des industries
animales en Guinée," <u>R. A.</u>, 1 (1962), pp. 5-10.

O'Connor, Michael.  "Guinea and the Ivory Coast:  Contrast
in Economic Development," <u>Journal of Modern Afri-</u>
<u>can Studies,</u> X, No. 3 (October, 1972), pp. 409-426.

Plazanet, Claude.  "L'Aide étrangère à la Guinée se chiffre
théoriquement à 180 millions de dollars," <u>Europe-</u>
<u>France-outre-mer,</u> no. 399 (April, 1963), pp. 14-17.

"Les Recherches minières de Guinée:  le Diamant," <u>Revue</u>
<u>du développement économique,</u> no. 4 (November, 1964),
pp. 11-13.

"La Réglementation domaniale depuis 1958 et les conséquences
du nouveau régime," <u>Revue du développement économ-</u>
<u>ique,</u> no. 4 (1964), pp. 9-10.

<u>Revue des Marchés Tropicaux et Méterranéens.</u>  Paris (week-
ly).

"Richesses minières et agricoles de la Guinée," <u>A. O. F. Mag-</u>
<u>azine,</u> no. 3 (November, 1953), 76 p. in-fol.

Rivière, Claude.  "Les Conséquences de la réorganisation
des circuits commerciaux en Guinée," <u>R. F. E. P. A.</u>,
No. 66 (June, 1971), pp. 74-96.

————.  "Les Coopératives agricoles en Guinée," <u>R. F. E.</u>
<u>P. A.</u>, No. 59 (November, 1970), pp. 55-64.

Salvadori, R.  "Esplorazione pratica della Guinea francese,"
<u>Africa,</u> 10 (1955), pp. 115-119.

————.  "Promuoviamo in Africa la collaborazione del
lavoro," <u>Africa,</u> 10 (1955), pp. 147-148.

Suret-Canale, Jean.  "Fria, établissement industriel guinéen,"
<u>R. A.</u>, nos. 2-3 (1963), pp. 3-27.

————.  "Fria, un exemple d'industrialisation africaine,"
<u>A. G.</u>, LXXIII (1964), pp. 172-188.

_____. "Notes sur l'économie guinéenne," Economie et politique, no. 123 (October, 1964), pp. 74-96.

_____. "Quelques Données statistiques sur la Guinée," R. A., 2 (1960), pp. 74-80.

Swindell, Kenneth. "Industrialization in Guinea," Geography, 54, No. 245 (November, 1969), pp. 456-458.

_____. "Iron ore mining in West Africa: some recent developments in Guinea, Sierra Leone and Liberia," Economic Geography, vol. 43, 4 (October, 1967), pp. 333-346.

Touré, Ismaël. "L'Avenir économique de la Guinée," Revue du développement économique, no. 3 (November, 1963), pp. 2-3.

Touré, M. Lamine. "Les Ports de Guinée," R. A. (1959), pp. 63-69.

_____. "Les Ressources hydro-électriques de la République de Guinée," R. A., no. 1 (1968), pp. 42-50.

Vidailhet, J. "La Future Industrie de l'aluminium en Guinée," Revue économique française, LXX, 2 (May, 1967), pp. 23-25.


GOVERNMENT DOCUMENTS

France. Institut National de la Statisque et des Etudes Economiques. Compendium des Statisques du Commerce Extérieur des pays Africains et Malgache. Paris: ann., 1957.

_____. Secrétariat d'Etat aux Relations avec les Etats de la Communauté. Aspects économiques et financiers du projet de Fria. Paris: French Government, 1961. Mech. dup.

Guinea. [République de Guinée.] Huitième Congrès du Parti démocratique de Guinée (RDA), tenu à Conakry du 25 septembre au 20 octobre 1967. Conakry: Imprimerie Nationale Patrice Lumumba, n. d.

_____. Plan comptable national et textes d'application.

Conakry: Impr. Nat. Patrice-Lumumba, 1965.

_____. Banque Nationale de Développement Agricole. "Rapport sur le fonctionnement et l'activité de banque nationale de développement agricole. " Exercice, 1965-1966.

_____. Ministère du Développement Economique. Huit années de développement économique. Conakry: 1967.

_____. Ministère du Domain Economique. Revue du développement économique. Conakry: 1964- .

_____. Ministre de la Fonction Publique et du Travail. Assemblée Nationale. Exposé fait le 25 octobre 1963 par le Ministre de la Fonction Publique et du Travail. Conakry: n. d. Mech. dup.

United States. Agency of International Development. Statistics and Development Division. Africa: Economic Growth Trends. Washington, D. C. : ann. , 1969+.

_____. Arms Control and Disarmament Agency. World Military Expenditures, 1971. Washington, D. C: G. P. O. , July, 1972.

_____. _____. World Military Expenditure and Arms Trade, 1963-1973. Washington, D. C: G. P. O. , 1975.

_____. Department of Commerce. Office of International Marketing. Market Profiles for Africa (Overseas Business Reports, OBR 72-074). Washington, D. C: G. P. O. , December, 1972.

_____. Department of Health, Education, and Welfare. Social Security Programs Throughout the World. Washington, D. C: G. P. O. , 1973.

_____. Department of State. Bureau of Intelligence and Research. Communist States and Developing Countries: Aid and Trade in 1973 (Research Studies No. INR RS-20). Washington, D. C: October 10, 1974.

_____. _____. _____. World Strength of Communist Party Organization, 1971. Washington, D. C: 1971.

_____. _____. _____. World Strength of Communist

Party Organization, 1972. Washington, D. C: 1972.

## DISSERTATIONS

Baldé, O. D. "La Portée de la loi-cadre du 8 novembre 1964 dans le développement économique de la Guinée. " Unpublished dissertation, I. P. C. (E. S. A. ), 1966-67.

Barry, M. A. S. "Contribution à l'étude des techniques et des méthodes de planification de l'économie guinéenne. " Unpublished dissertation, I. P. C. , 1969-70.

Bokoum, B. "Importance des entreprises d'Etat dans l'économie guinéenne. " Unpublished dissertation, I. P. C. (E. S. A. ), 1969-70.

Diallo, Tierno Nabica. "Bilan et perspectives de la Coopération dans le développement de l'agriculture guinéenne. " Unpublished dissertation, I. P. C. (E. S. A. ), 1967. Mech. dup.

Olémou, M. P. "Organisation et évolution des institutions du travail, République de Guinée. " Unpublished dissertation, I. P. C. (E. S. A. ), 1967-68.


## 7 EDUCATION


## BOOKS

Grange, Christiane. Géologie. Conakry: Ministère de l'Education Nationale, 1962.

Kitchen, Helen (ed. ). The Educated African. New York: Praeger, 1962.

United Nations. Statistical Yearbook, 1973, 25th ed. . New York: UN Department of Economic and Social Affairs, Statistical Office, 1974.

_____. Educational, Scientific and Cultural Organization. World Survey of Education, V: Educational Policy, Legislation, and Administration. Paris: UNESCO, 1971.

## ARTICLES

Adamolekun, 'Lapido. "Administrative Training in the Republic of Guinea, 1975-1970," Journal of Administration Overseas, XI, No. 4 (October, 1972), pp. 233-252.

Benot, Yves. "La Réforme de l'enseignement," Europe, no. 378 (October, 1960), pp. 116-127.

Camara, Djigui. "A la veille des examens de fin de cycle dans nos CER," Horoya, No. 2124 (June 20, 1974), p. 4.

Conté, Sendou. "Discours d'ouverture du séminaire des enseignants organisé à l'Institut polytechnique de Conakry," Revue R. D. A., 10 (1966), p. 6.

"Decret No. 0047 PRG du 8 Mars 1974," Journal Officiel de la République de Guinée, 16th year, No. 5 (March 1, 1974), pp. 64-66.

Diallo, Alpha Amadou. "Die Gründung eines Institutes für traditionelle Heilkunde," Afrika Heute, No. 14 (July 15, 1967), pp. 217-218. (In German.)

Diop, David Mandessi. "Autour de la réforme de l'enseignement en Guinée," P. A., XXIX (December, 1959-January, 1960), pp. 105-108.

Doré, Michel Blecko. "Institut Polytechnique de Kankan," Horoya (December 20, 1973), p. 3.

Du Bois, Victor D. "Guinea Educates a New Generation," Africa Report, VI, No. 7 (July, 1961), pp. 3-4, 8.

Pretty, Margaret. "L'Education en Guinée, 1878-1962," West African Journal of Education, XII, No. 2 (June, 1968), pp. 134-136.

"Recommandations du Conseil Supérieur de l'Education," Horoya, No. 1993 (April 28, 1973), pp. 2-3.

"Révolution culturelle en Guinée: Création de Centre d'Enseignement Révolutionnaire," Afrique Nouvelle, No. 1097 (August 15-21, 1968), p. 4.

Rivière, Claude. "Les Investissements éducatifs en République de Guinée, " C. E. A. , no. 20 (1965), pp. 618-634.

Stern, T. Noel. "Political Aspects of Guinean Education, " Comparative Education Review, VIII, No. 1 (June, 1964), pp. 98-103.

"Les Travaux du CNR: Rapport de la Commission de la Culture et de l'Education, " Horoya, Nos. 1925 and 1926 (August 18-21, 1972).

Weinstein, Brian. "Guinea's School of Public Administration, " Journal of Local Administration Overseas, IV, No. 4 (October, 1968), pp. 239-243.

GOVERNMENT DOCUMENTS

Guinea. Secretariat d'Etat à l'Idéologie, au Télé-Enseignement et à l'Alphabétisation. Les Budgets. Séminaires de formation professionnelle, Conakry: Centre de diffusion Télé-Enseignement, 1$^{er}$ trimestre, 1970. Mech. dup.

_____. _____. Gestion de l'entreprise. Responsabilité du comptable, Conakry: Centre de diffusion Télé-Enseignement, 2$^{ième}$ trimestre, 1970. Mech. dup.

_____. _____. Le Phénomène de l'échange, Conakry: Centre de Diffusion Télé-Enseignement, 2$^{ième}$ trimestre, 1970. Mech. dup.

_____. _____. Problèmes monétaires et cours des comptes, Conakry: Centre de diffusion Télé-Enseignement, 1$^{er}$ trimestre, 1970. Mech. dup.

United States. Educational Development in Guinea, Mali, Senegal, and Ivory Coast, by Bolibaugh, Jerry B. Washington, D. C: G. P. O. , 1972.

8 SCIENTIFIC STUDIES

BOOKS

Bonnet, P. , Vidal, P. , and Vérot, P. Premiers Résultats

des parcelles expérimentales d'études de l'érosion de
Sérédou en Guinée forestière. Dakar: n. d.

Christoffer, Erich. Aménagement du bassin du fleuve Sénégal. Les barrages et leurs incidences et aménagements hydro-électriques. Genève: Publications des
Nations Unies, 1963. ms.

Daget, J. Les Poissons du Fouta Dialon et la Basse Guinée.
(Mémoires de I. F. A. N., No. 65). Dakar: I. F. A. N.,
1962.

Dollfus, O. Essai morphologique sur la presqu'île du Kaloum et les îles de Los. Paris: Bibliothèque de l'Institut de géographie de Paris, n. d. ms.

Frohlich, Gerd. Guinea nach der Regenzeit. Leipzig:
Brockhous, 1961.

Grebaut, S., and Brengues, Jacques. Rapport de la mission
Commission de Cooperation Technique en Afrique sur
la trypanosomiase dans les territoires Kissis et dans
les régions frontières limitrophes en Guinée, Sierra
Leone et Libéria, April-June, 1964, O. R. S. T. O. M.
Mission entomologique auprès de l'Organisation de
Coopération contre les Grandes Endemies. Bobo-Diou-
lasso: 1964. Mech. dup.

Hance, William A. The Geography of Modern Africa. New
York: Columbia University Press, 1964.

Houis, M. La Guinée française. Paris: Editions géogra-
phiques, maritimes et coloniales, 1953.

Jamme, Gabriel. Mission d'étude de l'aménagement hydraulique de la zone côtière de la Guinée française, Rapport du chef de mission. Paris: Bulletin du Comité
d'études d'outre mer, 1952. Mech. dup.

Le Barbier, L. La Vallée du Moyen-Niger et la Haute-Guinée. Paris: Dujarric, 1904.

Leclerc, J.-C., Richard-Molard, J., Lamotte, M., Rougerie,
G., and Portères, R. La Chaine du Nimba, essai
géographique, Memoire I. F. A. N., no. 43 (La réserve
naturelle intégrale du mont Nimba, t. III). Dakar:

I. F. A. N. , 1955.

Le Cochec, F.   Rapport de Tournée dans le Samoh, à Kaback
    et à Kakossa.   Koba:   Centre Rizicole du Koba.   Koba,
    1956.   Mech.   dup.

Maignien, Roger.   Le Cuirassement des sols en Guinée, mém-
    oires du service de la carte géologique d Alsace et de
    Lorraine, no. 16.   Strasbourg:   1958.

May, Jacques Meyer, and McLellan, Donna L.   The Ecology
    of Malnutrition in the French-Speaking Countries of
    West Africa and Madagascar.   New York: Hafner, 1968.

Mountjoy, Alan B. , and Embleton, Clifford.   Africa:  A New
    Geographical Survey.   New York:  Praeger, 1967.

Phillips, John.   Agriculture and Ecology in Africa.   New York:
    Praeger, 1960.

Roche, Marcel, and Chartier, Roger.   Rapport préliminaire
    aux études hydrologiques.   Bassins expérimentaux des
    Timbis.   Paris:   O. R. S. T. O. M. , 1963.   Mech. dup.

Rouard de Card.   Traités de délimitation concernant l'Afri-
    que française.   Paris:   Pédone, 1900 (suppl. , Paris,
    Pédone, 1913.

_____.   Les Traités de protectorat conclus par la France
    en Afrique (1870-1895).   Paris:  Pédone, 1897.

Schnell, R.   La Fôret dense.   Paris:  Lechavalier, 1950.

United Nations.   Demographic Yearbook, 1959.   New York:
    UN Department of Economic and Social Affairs, Sta-
    tistical Office, 1959. _____, 1973.  1974.

_____.   Production Yearbook, 1972.   Rome:   United Na-
    tions Food and Agriculture Organization, 1973.

_____.   Survey on the Scientific and Technical Potential
    of the Countries of Africa.   Paris:  U. N. E. S. C. O. ,
    1970.


ARTICLES

Abbayes, H. des.   " Lichens récoltés en Guinée française et

en Côte d'Ivoire. III. Physciacées," Bull. I. F. A. N. ,
13 (1951), pp. 749-761.

_____. IV. Parméliacées," Bull. I. F. A. N. ,
13 (1951), pp. 965-977.

_____. V. Genres: Roccella, Coenogonium,
Sticta, Cladonia, Ramalina," Bull. I. F. A. N. , 14
(1952), pp. 19-27.

_____. VI. Collémancées, Heppiacées, Pan-
nariacées," Bull. I. F. A. N. , 14 (1952), pp. 450-456.

_____. VII. Pyrénulacées, Trypéthéliacées,
Astrothéliacées, Cyphéliacées," Bull. I. F. A. N. , 15
(1953), pp. 48-58.

_____, Alston, A. H. G. , and Tardieu-Blot, M. L. "Con-
tribution à la flore des Ptéridophytes d'A. O. F. (Guinée et Côte d'Ivoire)," Bull. I. F. A. N. , 13 (1951),
pp. 79-86; 15 (1953), pp. 1384-1386.

_____, and Motyka, J. "Lichens récoltés en Guinée fran-
çaise et en Côte d'Ivoire," Bull. I. F. A. N. , 12 (1950),
pp. 601-610.

Adam, J. "La Végétation de la source du Niger," A. G.
(July-September, 1947), pp. 192-200.

Arnould, Michel, Aymé, J.-M. , and Guillaume, R. "Nouvelle Stratigraphie des séries primaires du Nord du
Fouta-Djalon (Guinée-Sénégal)," C. R. S. S. G. F. , fasc.
7 (1959), pp. 166-167.

Balachowsky, A. S. "Deux Pseudaonidia Ckll. (Hom. Coc-
coidea-Diaspidinae) nouveaux du massif du Béna (Moy-
enne Guinée) A. O. F. ," Bull. I. F. A. N. , 15 (1953),
pp. 1512-1522.

Balandier, G. "L'Or de la Guinée française," P. A. , no. 4,
1ré serie (1948), pp. 539-548.

_____. "Toponymie des îles de Kabak et Kakossa," E. G. ,
no. 8 (1952), pp. 45-54.

Barry, Sory. "La Chasse en Guinée," R. A. , no. 1 (1960),
pp. 51-57.

_____. "Le Problème de la conservation des sols en Guinée," R. A. (1959), pp. 70-75.

"La Bauxite et l'industrie de l'Aluminium," Industries et travaux d'outre-mer, no. 87 (February, 1961), pp. 123-129.

Bonnet, P., and Vidal, Prosper. "Les Premiers Travaux du secteur pilote de conservation et d'utilisation des sols du Milo (Guinée forestière)," IIIᵉ Conférence interafricaine des sols, vol. II (1959), pp. 659-670.

_____. "Protection contre l'érosion hydrologique assurée par diverses cultures en Guinée forestière," Journal d'agronomie tropicale et de botanique appliquée, vol. V, no. 10 (1958), pp. 627-637.

Champion, J., Dugain, F., Maignien, R., and Domergues, U. "Les Sols de bananeraies et leur amélioration en Guinée," Fruits, vol. 13, nos. 9-10 (1958), pp. 415-462.

Chételat, E. de. "Le Modelé latéritique de l'Ouest de la Guinée française," Revue de géographie physique et de géologie dynamique (1938).

Chevalier, Auguste. "Les Hauts Plateaux du Fouta-Djalon," A. G. (1909), pp. 253-261.

Colemansky, V. "Faune muscicole de Guinée forestière (Rhizopodes testacés)," R. A., 4 (1962), pp. 33-60.

"Contribution du service météorologique national au développement économique de la Guinée," Revue du développement économique, no. 4 (November, 1964), p. 16.

Corfec, J. le. "Notes sur le Canton Tanda-Kade (Cerle de Gaoual)," E. G., 8 (1952), pp. 13-39.

Cousturier, Lucie. "La Forêt du Haut-Niger," Cahiers d'aujourd'hui, no. 12 (1923).

Cuille, J. "Contribution à l'étude de l'ethologie de Cosmopolites sordidus Germ," E. G., 1 (1947), pp. 9-22.

Daget, J. "Caractéristiques des cours d'eau du Fouta-Djalon," doc. no. 7, IVᵉ Colloque sur l'hydrobiologie et les pêches en eau douce, Fort Lamy, Commission de Coopération Technique en Afrique--Conseil Scientifique pour l'Afrique au Sud du Sahara (May 4-10, 1961). Mech. dup.

Dars, René, Sougy, Jean, and Vogt, Jean. "Observations nouvelles sur le "Cambro-ordovicien" du plateau mandingue occidental," C. R. S. S. G. F. (1959), p. 65.

Daveau, S. "Principaux Types de paysages morphologiques des plaines et plateaux soudanais," Information géographique, no. 2 (1962), pp. 61-72.

_____. "Ruissellement et soutirage dans la haute vallée du Denkalé (Monts Loma), Sierra Leone," Bulletin de l'Association des géographes français, nos. 330-331 (1965), pp. 20-27.

"Décret No. 145 PRG du 2 Juillet 1973" [concerning the result of the December 1972 general population census], Journal Officiel de la République de Guinée, 15th year, No. 18 (September 1, 1973), 187.

"Décret No. 246 PRG du 20 Septembre 1972," [concerning the taking of a general population census], Journal Officiel de la République de Guinée, 14th year, No. 21 (November 1, 1972), 182.

Dekeyser, P. L. "Présence de Thos adustus en Guinée Française," Bull. I. F. A. N. , 13 (1951), pp. 371-375.

Diallo, Noumouké. "Le Service de l'élevage et des industries animales en Guinée," R. A. , no. 1 (January-March, 1962), pp. 5-10.

Dollfus, O. "Conakry en 1951-1952, étude humaine et économique," E. G. , nos. 10-11 (1952), pp. 3-111.

Dresch, Jean. "Dépôts de couverture et relief en Afrique occidentale française," Congrès international de géographie (1952), pp. 323-326.

_____. "Pénéplaines africaines," A. G. (April-June, 1947), pp. 125-137.

_____. "Pénéplaines en Afrique noire française" (rapport de la commission pour la cartographie des surfaces d'aplanissement) Congrès international de géographie (1949), pp. 140-148.

_____. "Plaines soudanaises," R. G. D. (1953), pp. 39-44.

Ducos, Pierre. "L'Elevage en Guinée et la structure gén-étique de la race N'Dama," Bull. I. F. A. N., serie A no. 3 (July, 1961), pp. 886-903.

Dugain, François, and Fauck, Roger. "Mesures d'érosion et de ruissellement en Moyenne-Guinée. Relations avec certaines cultures," C. R. IIIe Conférence interafri-caine des sols, vol. II (1959), pp. 597-600.

Eichenberger, J. Y. "L'Exploitation de la bauxite en Guinée française," Industries et Travaux d'outre-mer, no. 4 (March, 1954), pp. 156-160.

Fauck, R. "Matière organique et azote des sols de la Moy-enne-Guinée et relations avec les rendements des cul-tures," Comptes rendus de l'Académie d'agriculture française, Vol. 46 (1960), pp. 152-155.

Gallais, Jean. "La Riziculture de plaine en Haute-Guinée," A. G., no. 367 (1959), pp. 207-223.

Gautier, E. F. "Climatic and physiographic notes on French Guinea," The Geographical Review, 23 (1933), pp. 248-258.

Godfriaux, I., Lamotte, M., and Rougerie, G. "La série stratigraphique du Simandou (Guinée française)," C. R. A. S., t 245 (1957), pp. 2343-2346.

Golemansky, V. "Etudes sur la faune des rhizopodes de Guinée forestière," R. A., 3 (1962), pp. 3-24.

Hain, Werner von. "Die Landwirtschaft der Republik Guinea," Geographische Berichte, IX, No. 3 (1964), pp. 179-193.

Henry, L. "Données sur la population de la Guinée," Pop-ulation, XI, 3 (1956), pp. 554-562.

Hiernaux, C. -R., and Villiers, A. "Spelcologica africana. Etude préliminaire de six cavernes de Guinée," Bull. I. F. A. N., XVII-A, no. 3 (1955), pp. 926-946.

Jaeger, Paul. "Contribution à l'étude du modelé de la dorsale guinéenne. Les Monts Loma (Sierra Leone)," R. G. D. , IV (1953), pp. 105-113.

_____, and Adam, J. -G. "Aperçu sommaire sur la végétation de la région occidentale de la dorsale Loma-Man. La galerie forestière de la source du Niger," Bull. de la Société de botanique de France, 94, nos. 7-8 (1947), pp. 323-334.

Jeremine, E. "Etude des statuettes Kissiennes au point de vue mineralogique et pétrographique," J. S. A. , 15 (1945), pp. 3-14.

Karst, J. "L'Achèvement du projet de Boké," Industrie et Travaux d'Outre-Mer, XX, No. 242 (January, 1974), pp. 38-43.

Kayser, B. "La Démographie de l'Afrique occidentale et centrale," C. O. M. (1965), pp. 73-85.

Killian, C. "Contribution à l'etude de la biologie de quelques Utricularia tropicaux," Bull. I. F. A. N. , 15 (1953), pp. 72-82.

_____. "Germination et développement post-embryonnaire de Genlisea africana," Bull. I. F. A. N. , 13 (1951), pp. 1029-1036.

_____. "Mesures écologiques sur des végétaux types du Fouta-Djallon (Guinée Française) et sur leur milieu, en saison sèche," Bull. I. F. A. N. , 13 (1951), pp. 601-681.

_____. "Observations biologiques sur un Ascomycète, parasite du Cyathea Dregeri," Bull. I. F. A. N. , 13 (1951), pp. 1037-1050.

_____. "Observations sur l'écologie et les bescins édaphiques du Quinquina," Bull. I. F. A. N. , 15 (1953), pp. 901-971.

Lacroix, Alfred. "La Constitution minéralogique de l'archipel de Los (Guinée)," C. R. A. S. , t. 141 (1905), p. 948; t. 142 (1906), p. 681; t. 146 (1908), p. 213; t. 156 (1913), p. 653.

Lamotte, M. , and Rougerie, G.    "Les Apports allochtones
    dans la genèse des cuirasses ferrugineuses, " R. G. D. ,
    nos. 10, 11, 12 (1962), pp. 145-160.

_____.  "Coexistence de trois types de modelé dans les
    chaînes quartzitiques du Nimba et du Simandou (Haute-
    Guinée), " A. G. (1952), pp. 432-442.

_____.  "Les Niveaux d'érosion intérieurs dans l'Ouest
    africain, " R. A. , no. 4 (1961), pp. 51-70.

_____, Rougerie, G. , and Godfriaux, I.  "Les Accumula-
    tions de quartzite à minerai de fer dans la chaîne du
    Simandou (Guinée française), " C. R. A. S. , t 247, 3
    (1958), pp. 315-318.

_____, and Roy, R.  "Les Principaux Traits du peuple-
    ment animal de la prairie montagneuse du mont Nim-
    ba (Guinée), " R. A. , no. 1 (1962), pp. 11-30.

_____, and Zuber-Vogeli, M.  "Contribution à l'étude des
    Batraciens de l'Ouest africain.  Le développement lar-
    vaire de Rana oxyrhynchus gribinguiensis Angel, "
    Bull. I. F. A. N. , 15 (1953), pp. 178-184.

Lavau, G. de.  "Boké, Guinée française, " Annales Africaines
    (1958), pp. 245-258.

Leclerc, J. -C. , Lamotte, M. , and Richard-Molard, J.    "Ni-
    veaux et cycles d'érosion dans le massif du Nimba
    (Guinée française), " C. R. A. S. , t. 228 (1949), pp.
    1510-1512.

Legoux, Pierre.  "Les Péridotites de Conakry et du Kaloum
    (République de Guinée) et leur serpentinisation, " C. R.
    S. S. G. F. , Vol. 3 (1960), p. 51.

_____, and Percival, F. -G.  "Sur la structure des cuiras-
    ses latéritiques ferrugineuses de Conakry, " C. R. A. S. ,
    t. 248 (1959), pp. 2226-2228.

Lestrange, Monique de.  "La Population de la région de You-
    kounkoun en Guinée française, " Population (October-
    December, 1950), pp. 643-668.

Maignien, R.  "Le Fouta-Djalon dans l'Ouest Africain, " R. A. ,
    3 (1960), pp. 25-38.

_____ . "Les Sols du Fouta-Djalon," C. R. Colloque Commission de Coopération Technique en Afrique - Conseil Scientifique pour l'Afrique au Sud du Sahara sur
la conservation des sols (April 30-May 7, 1960).

Marshall, G. A. K. "New Curculionidae (Col.) from French
West Africa," Bull. I. F. A. N., 13 (1951), pp. 319-325.

Mathis, Dr. Maurice. "Le Problème du miel, de la cire et
des abeilles en Guinée française," Agronomie tropicale,
nos. 11-12 (November-December, 1949), pp. 605-613.

"Mécanisation de la riziculture autochtone en Haute-Guinée,"
Riz et riziculture, 1$^{er}$ trim. (1959), pp. 15-29.

Michel, P. "L'Evolution géomorphologique des bassins du
Sénégal et de la Haute-Gambie," R. G. D., nos. 5-12
(May-December, 1959), pp. 117-143.

Millot, Georges, and Dars, René. "L'Archipel des îles de
Los," C. R. S. S. G. F. (1959), p. 8.

Monod, T. "Sur une Podestémonacée nouvelle pour l'A. O. F.,"
Bull. I. F. A. N., 7 (1945), pp. 156-159.

Pelissier, P., and Rougerie, G. "Problèmes morphologiques
dans le bassin de Siguiri (Haut-Niger)," Bull. I. F. A. N.,
15 (1953), pp. 1-47.

"Les Petits Aménagements d'hydraulique agricole du Haut-
Niger (Guinée)," Agronomie tropicale, nos. 7-8 (July-
August, 1949), pp. 420-423.

Picot, J. "N'Zérékoré, Guinée française," Annales Africaines
(1958), pp. 273-286.

Pitot, A. "Sur l'anatomie de Psilotum triquetrum Sw.,"
Bull. I. F. A. N., 12 (1950), pp. 315-334.

Portères, M. R. "Le Problème de la restauration du Fouta-
Djalon," R. A., 3 (1960), pp. 49-57.

Portères, Roland. "Observations sur les possibilités de culture du soja an Guinée française," Bull. agronomique,
no. 1 (November, 1946), 62p.

Poujade, J. "Technologie," E. G., 2 (1947), pp. 85-89.

Pouquet, J.  "Altération de dolérites de la presqu'île du
Cap-Vert (Sénégal) et du plateau de Labé (Guinée française)," Bulletin de l'Association des géographes française, nos. 245-246 (1954), pp. 173-182.

_____ .  "Aspects morphologiques du Fouta-Djalon," Revue
de géographie alpine, XLIII (1955), pp. 231-245.

"Quelques Données statistiques sur la Guinée," R. A. , 2 (1961),
pp. 74-80.

"Rapport sur la protection des sols au Fouta-Djalon," R. A. ,
3 (1960), pp. 38-47.

"La Réserve naturelle intégrale et la station scientifique nationale des Monts Nimba," R. A. , 2 (1960), pp. 69-71.

Richard-Molard, J.  "Les Densités de population au Fouta-
Djalon et dans les régions environnantes," Congrès
international de géographie, t. II (1952), pp. 192-204.

Ristorcelli, M.  "Le traitement indigène de la trypanosomiase
chez les Peuls du Fouta-Djallon (Guinée française),
J. S. A. , 9 (1930), pp. 1-2.

Rivière, Claude.  "La Toponymie de Conakry et du Kaloum,"
Bull. I. F. A. N. , XXVIII-B, 3-4 (1966).

Rouanet, R.  "Le Problème de la conservation des sols en
Guinée," E. G. , 8 (1952), pp. 59-65.

Rougerie, Gabriel.  "Modelés et dynamique de savane en
Guinée orientale," R. A. , no. 4 (1961), pp. 24-50.

_____ , and Lamotte, M.  "Le mont Nimba," Bulletin de
l'Association des géographes français, nos. 226-228
(1952), pp. 113-120.

Sautter, G.  "Le Fouta-Djalon," Bulletin de la Société lang-
uedocienne de géographie, Montpellier, 2e serie, t.
XV, 1 (1944), pp. 3-76.

Schnell, R.  "Contribution préliminaire à l'étude botanique
de la Basse-Guinée française," E. G. , no. 6 (1950),
pp. 29-72.

_____ .  "Esquisse de la végétation côtière de la Basse-
Guinée francaise," IIe Conférence internationale des

Africanistes de l'Ouest (1947), vol. II, 1 (1950), pp.
201-214.

_____. "Etudes préliminaires sur la végétation et la
flores des hauts plateaux de Mali (Fouta-Djallon),"
Bull. I. F. A. N. , 12 (1950), pp. 905-926.

_____. "Les Forêts primitives de la Basse-Guinée fran-
çaise," Comptes rendus somm. des séances de la Société de biogéographie, no. 248 (1952), pp. 12-16.

_____. "Noms vernaculaires et usages indigènes de plantes
d'Afrique Occidentale," E. G. , 4 (1950), pp. 57-80.

_____. "Note sur les îlots forestiers reliques de la Basse-
Guinée française," C. R. A. S. , t. 225 (1947), pp. 254-
255.

_____. "Plantes nouvelles ou peu connues d'Afrique oc-
cidentale française (Guinée et Côte d'Ivoire)," Bull.
I. F. A. N. , 15 (1953), pp. 93-97.

Serand, J. -M. "Les Iles de Los (Guinée française)," La
Géographie, vol. 47 (1927), pp. 1-28.

Silverstov. "Eléments de géomorphologie de la Guinée et
ses principaux problèmes," R. A. , no. 4 (1963), pp.
51-67.

Sory, B. "Le Problème de la conservation des sols en Guinée," R. A. , 1-4 (1959), pp. 70-75.

"Statistics: Vital Rates," Population Index, XL, No. 3 (July,
1974), pp. 596-608.

T. , J. "Conditions des études statistiques en Guinée," E. G. ,
12 (1953), pp. 60-63.

Touré, L. "Les Ressources hydro-électriques de la République de Guinée," R. A. , 1 (1960), pp. 42-50.

Tuzet, O. et al. "Trichophytes et ciliés parasites intestin-
aux de Pachybolus sp. , Scaphiostreptus obesus Attems
et Termatodiscus nimbanus Attems (Myriapodes Diplo-
podes)," Bull. I. F. A. N. , 15 (1953), pp. 133-142.

United Nations. "Population and Vital Statistics: Data Available as of 1 October 1974," Population and Vital Statistics Report, XXVI, No. 4 (1974), pp. 6-7.

Vigneron, B. "Kindia, Guinée française," Annales africaines (1958), pp. 259-272.

Vogt, J. "Aspects de l'évolution géomorphologique récente de l'Ouest africain," A. G. (1959), pp. 193-206.


GOVERNMENT DOCUMENTS

France, Rapport de mission sur le Moyen-Konkouré, by Fritsch, Pierre. Dakar: Gouvernement Général de l'A. O. F., Service de l'Hydraulique, 1956. Mech. dup.

_____. "Observations nouvelles sur les alluvions inactuelles de Côte-d'Ivoire et de Haute-Guinée," Actes du LXXXIVe Congrès national des Sociétés savantes, section de géographie, Dijon: Ministère de l'Education Nationale, Comité des Travaux Historiques et Scientifiques, 1959, pp. 205-210.

_____. Etude Démographique par Sondage en Guinée (1954-1955). Paris: Ministère de la France d'Outre-Mer, 1956. Mech. dup.

_____. Documents et Statistiques, L'Enquête Démographique de Guinée, 1954-1955: Résultats Provisoires, Ministère de la France d'Outre-Mer. Paris: n. d.

_____. Etude Démographique par Sondage in Guinée, 1954-1955: Résultats Définitifs, I and II, Service des Statostoqies Chargé des Relations et de la Coopération avec les Pays d'Outre-Mer. Paris: n. d.

Germany. Länderberichte: Guinea, Statistisches Bundesamt, Series Allgemeine Statistik des Auslandes. Stuttgart: Kohlhammer, 1967.

United States. Agency for International Development. Africa Data Book. Washington, D. C: A. I. D., December, 1973.

_____. Department of Commerce. Bureau of the Census. World Population: 1973. Washington, D. C: 1973.

DISSERTATIONS

Bah, Alpha Amadou. "Les Transports en Guinée." Unpublished dissertation, I. P. C. (E. S. A.), 1967.

Chautard. "Etude sur la géographie physique et la géologie du Fouta-Djalon." Unpublished dissertation, Sorbonne, 1905.

9 RELIGION

BOOKS

Arnaud, R. L'Islam et la politique musulmane en A. O. F. Paris: Publications du Comité de l'Afrique Française, 1912.

Begries, Gouverneur. L'Islam en Guinée française. Paris: Centre de Hautes Etudes Administratives sur l'Afrique et l'Asie Modernes, 1954.

Cardaire, M. L'Islam et le terroir africain. Bamako: I. F. A. N., 1954.

Deschamps, H. Les Religions d'Afrique noire. Paris: P. U. F., 1960.

Diané, El Hadj Kabiné. Recueil des cinq piliers de l'Islam, 3rd ed. Conakry: I. N. R. D. G., 1964.

Feral, G. Notes sur l'Islam en Guinée française. Paris: Centre de Hautes Etudes Administratives sur l'Afrique et l'Asie Modernes, 1948.

Froelich, J. C. Les Musulmans d'Afrique noire. Paris: Orante, 1962.

Gouilly, A. L'Islam dans l'Afrique occidentale française. Paris: Larose, 1952

Lelong, M. -H. N'Zérékoré; L'evangile dans la forêt. Paris: Librairie missionnaire, 1949.

Lewis, I. M. (ed.). Islam in Tropical Africa. London:

Oxford University Press, 1966.

Marty, Paul. L'Islam en Guinée. Fouta-Djalon. Paris: Leroux, 1921.

Monteil, Vincent. L'Islam noir. Paris: Seuil, 1964.

Trimingham, J. Spencer. A History of Islam in West Africa. London: Oxford University Press, 1962.

## ARTICLES

"Cinquantenaire de la mission de Boffa," La Voix de Notre-Dame. Bulletin diocesain (July, 1927).

"Islam ou colonisation au Fouta-Djalon," P. A. , 15 (1953), pp. 357-364.

Le Grip, R. "Aspects actuels de l'Islam en A. O. F. , " L'Afrique et l'Asie, XXVIII (1954), pp. 43-61.

Maka, Léon. "Le P. D. G. et les religions," Horoya, No. 1238 (June 30, 1967).

Rivière, Claude. "Bilan de l'Islamisation," Afrique Documents, No. 5-6 (1960), pp. 319-359.

Suret-Canale, Jean. "Touba in Guinea: Holy Place of Islam," African Perspectives (1970), pp. 53-81.

Tchidimbo, Mgr. R. M. "L'Homme noir dans l'Englise," P. A. (1963), pp. 89-90.

Thomas, L. V. "L'Englise chrétienne d'Afrique noire," Tam-Tam (December 1, 1963), p. 10.

## 10 LITERATURE AND POETRY

### BOOKS

Brench, Anthony C. The Novelists' Inheritance in French Africa. London: Oxford University Press, 1967.

_____. Writing in French from Senegal to Cameroon.

London:  Oxford University Press, 1967.

Herdeck, Donald E.   African Authors:  A Companion to Black
African Writing, 1300-1973.  Washington:  Black Orpheus Press, 1973.

Jahn, Janheinz.   Who's Who in African Literature.  Tübingen:
Horst Erdmann Verlag, 1972.

Zell, Hans, and Silver, Helene (eds. ).   A Reader's Guide to
African Literature.   New York:  Africana Publishing
Company, 1971.


ARTICLES

Appia, B.   "Quelques Proverbes guinéens, "  Bull. I. F. A. N. ,
2 (1940), pp. 396-415.

B. , A.   "L'Enfant noir, "  P. A. , 16 (1954), pp. 419-420.

Balandier, G.   "Toponymie des Iles de Kabak et Kakossa, "
E. G. , 8 (1952), pp. 49-54.

Cesair, A.   "Salut à la Guinée, "  P. A. , N. S. 26 (1959), p.
89.

Cessain, M.   "La Littérature orale des Coniagui (République
de Guinée), "  R. A. , 3 (1961), pp. 24-37; 3 (1962), pp.
25-50.

"Chants révolutionnaires guinéens, "  P. A. , N. S. 29 (1959-
1960), pp. 89-103.

Henebelle, Guy.   "Côte d'Ivoire, Sénégal, Guinée:  six ciné-
astes Africains parlent, "  L'Afrique Littéraire et Artistique, No. 8 (December, 1969), pp. 58-70.

Houis, M.   "Caractères et possibilités de la langue Soso, "
R. A. , 1 (1962), pp. 3-4.

_____.   "Contes Baga, "  E. G. , 6 (1950), pp. 3-15.

_____.   "Notes lexicologiques sur les rapports du soso
avec les langues màde-dud du groupe mana-busa, "
Bull. I. F. A. N. , 16 (1954), pp. 391-401.

_____. "Le Rapport d'annexion en baga," Bull. I. F. A. N.,
15 (1953), pp. 848-854.

_____. "Le Système pronominal et les classes dans les
dialectes baga," Bull. I. F. A. N., 15 (1953), pp. 381-
404.

Joffre, J.   "Sur un nouvel alphabet ouest-africain le Toma
(frontière franco-libérienne)," Bull. I. F. A. N., 7
(1945), pp. 160-173.

Lassort. "La Langue Kpèlè," E. G., 2 (1947), pp. 21-25.

Laye, Camara.   "The Eyes of the Statue," Black Orpheus,
V (1959), pp. 19-27.

Mamadou, S.   "Contes et légendes d'Afrique," R. A., 2
(1961), pp. 30-44.

"Un mariage chez les Mandegnis," P. A., 4 (1948), pp. 637-
640.

Mengrelis, T.   "Contes de la forêt," E. G., 5 (1950), pp.
3-6.

_____. "Curiosités linguistiques," Africa, 21 (1951),
p. 138.

_____. "Deux Contes toma," E. G., 1 (1947), pp. 27-45.

Poreko, D. O.   "A propos des phonèmes spéciaux de la langue Peule," R. A., 4 (1960), pp. 37-39.

Porteres, P.   "Notes de toponymie rurale au Fouta-Djallon,"
R. A., 1-4 (1964), pp. 151-159.

Sissoko, F. D.   "Glossaire des mots français passés en Malinké," Bull. I. F. A. N., 1 (1939), pp. 325-366.

Sow, A. I.   "Notes sur les procédés poétiques dans la littérature des Peuls du Fouta-Djalon," C. E. A., 5 (1965),
pp. 370-385; P. A., N. S. 54 (1965), pp. 181-197.

"Three Soussou tales [Sweetness, The Moon, The Well],
Black Orpheus, XV (1964), p. 5

## 11 LINGUISTICS

### BOOKS

Delafosse, Maurice. La Langue mandingue et ses dialectes.
Paris: Geuthner, 1929.

Greenberg, Joseph H. The Languages of Africa, 3rd ed.
Bloomington: Indiana University, 1970.

Heine, Bernard. Status and Use of African Lingua Franca.
Munich: Weltforum Verlag, 1970.

### ARTICLES

Conil-Lacoste, Michel, and Tracoré, Kamori. "No More
Secret Languages," New Africa, IX, No. 3-4 (1967),
p. 14.

Hair, P. E. H. "Ethnolinguistic Continuity on the Guinea Coast, "
Journal of African History, VIII, No. 2 (1967), pp.
247-268.

## 12 ART AND MUSIC

### BOOKS

Bravmann, René A. Islam and Tribal Art in West Africa.
London: Cambridge University Press, 1974.

Hennebelle, Guy, et al. (eds.). Les Cinémas Africains en
1972. Paris: Société Africaine d'Edition, 1972.

Laude, Jean. The Arts of Black Africa. Berkeley: University of California Press, 1971.

Leuzinger, Elsy. Africa: The Art of the Negro Peoples,
translated by Ann E. Keep, 2d ed. New York: Crown,
1967.

Teel, William. An Outline of African Art. Cambridge,
Mass.: University Prints, 1970.

ARTICLES

Diaré, Ibrahim Khalil. "Musique guinéenne: audience et
prestige," Horoya, No. 2098 (March 24, 1974), p. 7.

_____. "Les Orchestres modernes aux compétitions ré-
gionales," Horoya, No. 1935 (September 28, 1972),
p. 2.

"Les Films guinéens remportent la médaille d'or," Horoya,
No. 1979 (March 11, 1973), p. 2.

"French Guinea," Encyclopedia of World Art (1959), pp. 56-
58.

Germain, J. "Extrait d'une monographic des habitants du
cercle de N'Zérékoré (Guerzé, Kono, Manon). Les
Artisans les techniques et les arts," E. G., 13 (1955),
pp. 3-54.

Knight, Roderic. "Record Reviews (Musique malinké: Guinée; and Musique d'Afrique occidentale: Musique malinké, musique baoulé)," Ethnomusicology, XVIII, No.
2 (May, 1974), pp. 337-339.

Okpaku, Joseph. "Les Ballets Africains Sont Belles: Guinea's National Ensemble in San Francisco," Journal
of the New African Literature and the Arts, Issue No.
Fall 1967 (June, 1968), pp. 65-67.

Rouget, G. "Les Ballets africains de Keita Fodeba," P. A.,
N. S. 7 (1956), pp. 138-140.

Sano, M. "De la mélodie populaire Alpha Yaya, à l'hymne
national Liberté," R. A., 2-3 (1963), pp. 28-32.


GOVERNMENT DOCUMENTS

Guinea. Le Haut Commissariat à l'Information au Tourisme
et à L'I. N. R. D. G. Chefs d'Oeuvre de l'Art Guinéen
et Africain: Catalogue, Conakry: Institut National de
Recherches et de Documentation, 1967.

## 13 TOURISM

BOOKS

Greene, Graham. Journey Without Maps, 2nd ed. New York: Viking, 1961 (1936).

ARTICLES

Balachowsky, A. S. "Le Fouta-Djalon," La Nature, no. 3227 (March, 1954), pp. 83-88.

_____. "La Guinée forestière et les monts Nimba," La Nature, no. 3229 (May, 1954), pp. 161-167.

_____. "Le Pays mandêni en Basse-Guinée," La Nature, no. 3215 (March, 1953), pp. 65-68.

Barry, S. "Le Chasse en Guinée," R. A., 1 (1960), pp. 51-57.

Diop, A. "Impressions de voyage," P. A., N. S. 29 (1959-1960), pp. 3-7.

GOVERNMENT DOCUMENTS

Guinea. Ministère de l'information et du tourisme. "Quatre Années d'indépendence et de liberté," Conakry: I. N. P. D. G., 1962.

_____. Office of the Secretary of State for Information and Tourism. "Guinea and Its People," Conakry: Office of the Secretary of State for Information and Tourism, 1965.

## 14 REFERENCE AND BIBLIOGRAPHY

BOOKS

Africa South of the Sahara, 6th ed. London: Europa Publications, 1976.

Almeida, Damien d'. Premier Repetoire des archives nationales de Guinée. Conakry: I. N. R. D. G. , 1962.

Annuaire des missions catholiques en Afrique française. Paris: Editions Paul Balsey-oep, 1955.

Asamani, J. O. Index Africances. Stanford, Calif.: Hoover Institution Press, 1975.

Bederman, Sanford H. Africa; A Bibliography of Geography and Related Disciplines, Atlanta: Georgia State University Press, 1974.

Bogaert, Jozef. Sciences humaines en Afrique noire: guide bibliographique (1945-1965). Bruxelles: Centre Documentation Economique et Sociale Africaine, 1966.

Booth, Richard. The Armed Forces of African States (Adelphi Papers no. 67). London: International Institute for Strategic Studies, 1970.

Brasseur, P. , and Maurel, J. F. Les Sources bibliographiques de l'Afrique de l'ouest et de l'Afrique équatoriale d'expression française. Dakar: Bibliothèque de l'Université, 1970.

Busch, Lawrence. Guinea, Ivory Coast and Senegal; A Bibliography on Development. Monticello, Ill.: Council of Planning Librarians, 1973.

Carson, P. Materials for West African History in French Archives. London: Athlone Press, 1968.

Conover, H. F. Official Publications of French West Africa, 1946-58. Washington, D. C: Library of Congress, 1960.

Désiré-Vuillemin, G. Les Capitales de l'ouest-africain, 2 vols. Paris: Service d'Etudes et de Recherches. Pédagogiques pour les Pays en Voie de Développement, 1963.

Dictionary of African Biography, 2nd ed. London: Melrose Press, 1971.

Duignan, Peter (ed. ). Guide to Research and Reference Works on Sub-Saharan Africa. Stanford, Calif.: Hoover Institution Press, 1971.

Dupuy, Trevor N. (ed. ). The Almanac of World Military

<u>Power.</u>  Dunn Loring, Va. :   T. N. Dupuy Associates, 1970.

European Economic Communities.  Statistical Office.  <u>Annu-aire Statistique des E. A. M. A.</u>  Luxembourg, ann. , 1969+.

_____.  _____.  <u>Foreign Trade Statistics.</u>  Associates Overseas Areas.  Brussels:  1959-65.

Frost, J. M.  (ed. ).  <u>World Radio-TV Handbook, 1974.</u>  Hvi-dovre, Denmark:  World Radio-TV Handbook, 1974.

Hoover Institution.  <u>U. S. and Canadian Publications and The-ses on Africa, 1961-1966.</u>  Stanford, Calif. :  Hoover Institution Press, n. d.

Kohler, Joehen.  <u>Deutsches Dissertationen über Afrika:  ein Verzeichnis für die Jahre 1918-1959.</u>  Bonn:  K. Schroeder für Deutsche Afrika-Gesselschaft, 1962.

Organisation de Coopération et de Développement Economique, Centre de Développement.  <u>Bibliographie de la Guinée.</u>  Paris:  Organisation de Coopération et de Développement Economique, Centre de Développement, 1965.

Panofsky, Hans E.  <u>A Bibliography of Africana.</u>  Westport, Conn. :  Greenwood Press, 1975.

Pick, Franz (ed. ).  <u>Pick's Currency Yearbook, 1973.</u>  New York:  Pick Publishing, 1973.

Ryder, A. F. C.  <u>Materials for West African History in Por-tuguese Archives.</u>  London:  Athlone Press, 1965.

Rydings, H. A.  <u>The Bibliographies of West Africa.</u>  Ibadan:  Ibadan University Press, 1961.

Standing Conference on Library Materials on Africa.  <u>United Kingdom Publications and Theses on Africa.</u>  Cam-bridge, England:  Heffer, 1963+.

Ternaux-Compans, Henri.  <u>Bibliothèque asiatique et africaine ou catalogue des ouvrages relatifs à l'Asie et à l'Af-rique, qui ont paru depuis la découverte de l'impri-merie jusqu'en 1700.</u>  Paris:  1841 (repr. :  Amster-dam:  B. H. Gruner, 1968).

Wieschnoff, Heinrich A.  Anthropological Bibliography of Africa.  New Haven, Conn. :  American Oriental Society 1948.

Witherel, Julian W.  French Speaking West Africa:  A Guide to Official Publications.  Washington, D. C. :  Library of Congress, 1967.


ARTICLES

Africa.  London (quarterly).

Afrique.  Casablanca (six times a year).

Afrique Nouvelle.  Dakar (weekly).

Année Africaine.  Paris (yearly).

Année Politique Africaine.  Dakar (yearly).

Autra, Ray (Mamadou Traoré)  "L'institut national de recherches et de documentation de la République de Guinée, " R. A. (1964), pp. 5-35.

Chronologie Politique Africaine.  Paris (bimonthly).

The Economist Intelligence Unit--Former French Tropical Africa.  London (quarterly).

Etudes Guinéennes.  Conakry (irregular).

Europe-France-Outre-Mer.  Paris (monthly, including the annual June survey of all African states).

Horoya.  Conakry (daily).

Horoya-Hebdo.  Conakry (weekly).

Jeune Afrique.  Paris (weekly).

Johnson, G. Wesley.  "The Archival System of Former French West Africa, " African Studies Bulletin, VIII, No. 1 (April, 1965), pp. 48-58.

Le Monde.  Paris (daily).

Marchês Tropicaux et Méditerranéens.   Paris (weekly).

Mauny, Raymond.  "Contribution à la bibliographie de l'histoire de l'Afrique noire des origines à 1850, " Bull.
I. F. A. N. , XXVII, No. 3-4 (July-October, 1966), pp.
927-965.

New York Times.   New York (daily).

Overseas Associates: Statistical Bulletin.   Brussels (5 is-
sues annually).

Washington Post.   Washington (daily).

West Africa.   London (weekly).

GOVERNMENT DOCUMENTS

France.  Institut National de la Statisque et des Etudes Economiques.  Compendium des Statisques du Commerce
Extérieur des pays de la Zone Franc, Paris (ann.,
1938?-1946?)

DISSERTATIONS

Kake, B.  Bibliographie critique des sources imprimées d'histoire de la Guinée.  Unpublished dissertation, Dakar:
1962.

MAPS

Mercier, Paul.  Carte Ethno-Démographique de l'Afrique Occidentale, No. 5 Dakar: I. F. A. N. , 1954, p. 4.

Richard-Molard, Jacques.  Cartes ethno-démographiques de
l'Afrique occidentale, Dakar: I. F. A. N. , 1952.